If you're traveling to the beach, pack your sunscreen. If you're heading for the mountains, don't forget your climbing boots. But if you're on the road to a deeper understanding of Scripture, get the best tour guide around: Lisa Harper. You won't get lost. You'll be captivated by the scenery. Most of all, you'll be glad you made the journey.

MAX LUCADO

Lisa has a wonderful gift. She can plunge into the depths of God's Word and extract diamonds of wisdom and grace for every hungry heart. I love to hear her speak but never more so than when she is leading a Bible study. This book will be like a breath of fresh air to your soul.

SHEILA WALSH
Women of Faith speaker and author of
Extraordinary Faith

on the road with
Lisa Harper

HOLDING OUT
for a HERO
a new spin on Hebrews

Tyndale House Publishers, Inc.
Wheaton, Illinois

Visit Tyndale's exciting Web site at www.tyndale.com

TYNDALE is a registered trademark of Tyndale House Publishers, Inc.

Tyndale's quill logo is a trademark of Tyndale House Publishers, Inc.

Holding Out for a Hero

Designed by Beth Sparkman

ISBN-13: 978-1-4143-0276-8

ISBN-10: 1-4143-0276-2

Printed in the United States of America

11   10   09   08   07   06   05
7   6   5   4   3   2   1

In loving memory of

Thomas "Michie" Hill

Michie loved his Savior, Jesus; his wife, Michele; his children, Kim, Jamie and his wife, Julie, Lacey and her husband, Andrew; his eight grandchildren; and other family members and friends too numerous to mention. He was also partial to fast driving, fair food, puzzles, planes, short lines, Scrabble, and jitterbugging. He ran the race of faith like a true champion and is now beholding a glory that you and I can only imagine. And we're pretty sure he's dancing.

CONTENTS

Author's Note

Recently I talked my friend Traci into giving sushi a second chance. She had tried it once before but had experienced unpleasant results. She wasn't too keen on another culinary adventure. But after I assured her there are some types of sushi that don't include raw fish, eels, octopuses, or other hapless sea creatures, she relented. We went to a small Japanese restaurant near my house, and I ordered several kinds of "sissy sushi"—my favorite of which is shrimp fried in tempura batter, then rolled in rice with fresh avocado slices. It's probably more fattening than an entire box of Krispy Kremes, but it sure is delicious! And it was fun to watch Traci's expression change from squeamish reluctance to surprised delight with one bite!

I often meet people whose experience with Bible studies is just as unpleasant as Traci's first date with sushi. I've heard stories about Bible teachers so dreary they seemed to be auditioning for a skit about funeral directors. One woman told me she stopped attending the study at her church because she and her friends just couldn't stop giggling at the "sea of bobbing heads" around them—the result of so many people falling asleep! Others talk about the drudgery of spending too much time in Leviticus or how they were made to feel like spiritual pygmies when they asked questions about something they

didn't understand in the lesson. Although some of the worst-case scenarios are humorous, it's not at all funny when people who are seeking a more intimate relationship with God end up thinking the Bible is boring, inexplicable, or irrelevant.

God's Word is anything but boring. This "book" is an exciting literary masterpiece! It's full of dramatic plots, engaging narrative, and beautiful poetry. It's also a book of stunning revelation, divine comfort, and tangible hope. It can be mysterious and difficult to decipher, but it's never dull. Those who have walked away from Bible studies with the impression that reading God's Word is tedious or futile have been misguided, usually by ineffectual leaders, monotonous teachers, or outdated methodologies.

The following chapters are an attempt to help people explore the Bible in a new way. This is an "outside the box" kind of Bible study. It isn't a verse-by-verse curriculum or an exhaustive commentary. My style is more like those wonderfully singable *Sound of Music* lyrics: These are a few of my favorite things!

In this book, we'll look at some of my favorite sections of Hebrews, which is actually a riveting New Testament sermon. We'll read funny stories and consider relevant illustrations to help clarify the murky points. We'll wrestle with some of those confusing passages that aren't so easy to tie up with a doctrinal ribbon. And throughout each chapter we'll ponder questions about how these ancient, supernatural words still affect us today.

I also hope you make use of the DVD that came with this book. It probably won't win an Oscar, but we think it's more interesting than most reality television, and it will help you to apply the lessons of Hebrews to your life today. You'll meet a small group of my friends as we gather in my living room to discuss key questions from each chapter. I think you'll find that the interaction is often poignant, sometimes humorous, and always authentic—just like my friends. I hope you'll watch it with your own group of friends, or by yourself, and consider how you would respond to the points made and the issues raised in our conversations.

While this book is technically a Bible study, it doesn't have to be a stereotypical Bible study. I'll be thrilled if you use it in Sunday school, small groups, and women's ministry settings. But I also hope you will invite friends, neighbors, and even your mother-in-law to discuss it in your book club after you finish Oprah's latest selection! I hope people who wouldn't darken the door of a church or participate in a conventional Bible study will read it in Starbucks or watch the DVD in their own living room. And I hope by taking the risk to read a "Christian" book, they'll get a clearer picture of who God is and realize that He's the "hero" they've been searching for.

Lisa

PS: As you work your way through the book, you'll notice that certain questions have a DVD **DVD** symbol next to them. Whenever you see this symbol, pop in the enclosed DVD, cue up the right chapter, hit play, and see what my book club had to say about Hebrews.

Watch as you go, do a chapter at a time, or make a night out of it and watch all of the questions at once. Enjoy!

Holding Out for a Hero

Where have all the good men gone
And where are all the gods?
Where's the streetwise Hercules
To fight the rising odds?
Isn't there a white knight upon a fiery steed?
Late at night I toss and I turn and I dream of what I need

I need a hero
I'm holding out for a hero 'til the end of the night
He's gotta be strong
And he's gotta be fast
And he's gotta be fresh from the fight
I need a hero
I'm holding out for a hero 'til the morning light
He's gotta be sure
And it's gotta be soon
And he's gotta be larger than life
Larger than life[1]

Introduction

A few years ago I went through a mini midlife crisis and became the proud owner of a black motorcycle. My insurance premiums shot up, along with a lot of church members' eyebrows. I think most women—especially Christian women—have an innate suspicion of Harley Davidsons. My hypothesis isn't based on scientific data, but on lots of personal experience.

There's just something about my bike and black leather jacket that causes minivan-driving moms to frown in disapproval. It's interesting to watch their reaction at intersections. Judging from their expressions, you would think I was sitting there naked, chugging a bottle of whiskey, with a big tattoo declaring "Reprobates Rule"! But contrary to their assumptions about my morality, I'm often riding to a Bible study. A few times I've even had the delight of roaring up behind one of those highway critics in the church parking lot.

To be fair, I have met a few motorcycle fans in Christian circles. One pastor even asked if I would ride in on his Harley Road King when he introduced me at his church's women's retreat. He thought the women in his congregation needed to loosen up a little, and he assumed my entrance on a big blue bike with black fringe streaming from the handlebars would begin the process! Since he *was* the pastor, and it *was* his idea, I

agreed to the stunt. While I sat there idling in the church foyer—wondering if my career as a retreat speaker was over—he leaned toward me and said, "Just ride it straight down the middle aisle, then turn right, and park by the altar." His request ranks right up there as one of the most unusual things I've ever been asked to do by a minister!

But for the most part, I've experienced more grief than grace in regards to my two-wheeled proclivity, because motorcycles aren't considered an appropriate mode of transportation for female Bible teachers. Several cropped-pants-wearing Pharisees have made that point crystal clear! They think I should wear linen, not leather, and bake casseroles instead of burning rubber.

The New Testament book of Hebrews ("Hebrew" is a common term for "Jew" or "Jewish") was written to a group of Jewish believers who were kind of like me on a motorcycle—they just didn't fit in.

Who would've thought Harleys and Hebrews had anything in common?

1

Danger Ahead

Jewish Christians living in the first century didn't have to zoom around on Harleys to stick out like sore thumbs: everything they did was contrary to their culture. They were monotheistic—they believed in one God, Jehovah—while the religious climate of their day was much less discriminating. When Paul said, "Gentlemen, I can see that you are very religious," he wasn't exaggerating.

> *So Paul, standing in the midst of the Areopagus, said: "Men of Athens, I perceive that in every way you are very religious. For as I passed along and observed the objects of your worship, I found also an altar with this inscription, 'To the unknown god.' What therefore you worship as unknown, this I proclaim to you."*
>
> Acts 17:22-23

Monotheism
the belief in one God

Polytheism
the belief in more than one god or theology

Syncretism
adhering to multiple creeds

This passage in Acts was written at about the same time as Hebrews. It highlights the culture of the day, which was polytheistic (multiple theologies) and syncretistic (multiple creeds). Greeks and Romans weren't antireligious—they were enthusiastic participants in every conceivable kind of religion. For instance, when Greece or Rome conquered another civilization, they just added that belief system to the ever-growing list. Rome had more than two hundred *god* statues on street corners, a diminutive "deity" guarding virtually every fork in the road.

did you know?

Although emperor worship was commonly practiced in the first century, history does reveal that most emperors didn't really believe they were literal gods. Few actually forced their subjects to adhere to emperor worship which included offering incense and prayers on their behalf. The whole incense thing was mostly political pomp and circumstance, not altogether different from the bumper sticker bonanza that happens every four years prior to presidential elections in America. But there were a few loony rulers who took the matter very seriously!

Emperor Domitian (AD 81–96) was as nutty as a fruitcake. He was so captivated by the idea that he was actually a god, he ordered people killed if they didn't call him "Lord." Nuttier still was the egomaniacal emperor Caligula (AD 37–41). Caligula insisted he was supernatural to the extent that he ordered soldiers to place his image inside the Temple in Jerusalem. The Jews objected to his audacious heresy and staged a revolt. As a protest, they refused to farm their land, effectively demonstrating that they'd rather starve than worship him alongside Jehovah. Of course, this caused long lines in the grocery store—making all the housewives mad—and Caligula responded by decreeing that all Jews be put to death (brings to mind another nut named Hitler, doesn't it?). Fortunately, he was overthrown before his murderous scheme could be carried out.[1]

**Read Acts 17:22-34 for the full account of
Paul's discussion with the hedonistic Greeks in
Athens. What can you pick up about their
culture in light of Paul's clarifications? Do you
know anyone who worships an "unknown" god?**

Even Jewish religious leaders gorged themselves
at the counterfeit faith buffet, with some priests
officiating at several different types of religious
ceremonies. Can you imagine if a pastor preached
at your church on Sunday morning—espousing
biblically sound doctrine—then put on a robe and
sashayed over to the Islamic center on Friday
night to preside over their services?

Another interesting ingredient of this religious
smorgasbord was emperor worship. All Roman
citizens were legally required to show loyalty to
the current political leader several times a year by
putting a pinch of incense on an altar and praying
to or for the emperor.[2] We've observed a modern
spectacle of emperor worship on our TV news in
the past few years through the plethora of bill-
boards, statues, and buildings dedicated to Saddam
Hussein. Much like those ancient taxpayers, some
Middle Easterners still find it personally benefi-
cial—even necessary—to affirm that their dictator
is also a "god."

Something Old, Something New

In spite of the challenges of the day, Judaism was
still largely tolerated throughout the Roman Empire
in the first century—perhaps because there were 3
to 4 million Jews, most of whom were religious and

believed that Jehovah was the one, true God, but *didn't* believe that Jesus was the promised Messiah the Old Testament spoke of—and it would have been a political nightmare to prohibit them from worshipping. Also, the Jews were rarely civilly disobedient; they didn't really bother anyone. And lastly, Judaism was an ancient religion, and the Romans were enamored with old things.

But Jews who had embraced Christianity were a whole new ball game.

Christianity was suspicious because it was brand-new. Plus it was growing like wildfire, which made it even more dubious. It was considered dangerous because its followers were intolerant of other religions, insisting that some guy named Jesus was the only liaison to the one true God. And to make matters much worse, there had been a huge misunderstanding about the sacraments. When Christian converts talked about "eating His body and drinking His blood," people thought they were practicing cannibalism. Neighbors of confessing Christians started eyeing them with suspicion and panicked every time a Jewish believer invited them to a barbecue!

Have you ever been in one of those matching-purse-and-shoes Christian settings where you felt that you stuck out like a sore thumb? How did you respond?

And these cheeky Christians didn't capitulate in order to go with the cultural flow. Their morals made it nearly impossible to live an under-the-radar existence. They believed in the concept of family—marriage between a man and a woman, and if they were blessed, a house filled with children. But in Greco-Roman society, husbands and wives were like the pants in my closet that actually fit: few and far between! Not many people got married in those days—usually only the wealthy, for reasons of property disbursement. Fewer still practiced monogamy.

While abortion was frowned on (Greek mysticism gave them a healthy fear of homicide), babies were often abandoned. Especially little girls. Infants were set on the side of the road like trash. The surviving girls usually became cult prostitutes, and the boys ended up in gladiatorial schools, where they were trained to fight. Archaeologists have uncovered the ruins of massive coliseums where hundreds of gladiators in a single day would fight to the death for the purpose of "entertainment."[3]

But Christians didn't buy tickets to the kill-or-be-killed championships. They didn't party at the local bars. They swam against the tide and got married. They cherished their children. They didn't discard their daughters. They even rescued other people's babies from the edge of the interstate. They delivered chicken soup to pagans with the flu. They were the last in line and the first to serve. The Jewish Christians were quickly becoming the flies in their world's amoral ointment.

It's been said that Hebrews is like an eccentric millionaire: rich but puzzling. What questions have already formed in your mind about this bewildering book?

When the Going Gets Tough

Recall the former days when, after you were enlightened, you endured a hard struggle with sufferings, sometimes being publicly exposed to reproach and affliction, and sometimes being partners with those so treated. For you had compassion on those in prison, and you joyfully accepted the plundering of your property, since you knew that you yourselves had a better possession and an abiding one.

Hebrews 10:32-34

This passage makes it clear that it wasn't the first time these converts had faced an angry mob of

did you know?

Nero reigned from AD 54 to 68. Most scholars agree that Hebrews was written between the years 60 and 70, before the destruction of the second Temple, based on historical documents and textual references to the Temple and the sacrificial system. Remember there were technically two Jewish Temples: God gave David the vision for the first one, which was eventually built by his son, Solomon, around 960 BC. But that magnificent Temple was destroyed by one of Israel's enemies, the Babylonian king, Nebuchadnezzar, in 587 BC. Jewish exiles attempted to rebuild the Temple when they returned from captivity in Babylon (516 BC), but their restoration project fell woefully short of the Temple's original splendor.

Construction of the "second" Temple—also a major remodeling project—began in 20 BC and was completed in 26 AD. The forty-six-year Temple reconstruction project was commissioned by King Herod for political reasons and was considered the greatest building and engineering achievement of his reign. But that Temple was ultimately demolished as well. It was ransacked, razed, and set ablaze by Roman emperor Titus and his troops in AD 70 in their attempt to systematically destroy Jerusalem. Religious Jews still cling to the belief that when their messiah comes, he will literally build another glorious Temple in Jerusalem.

former friends and neighbors. They had been bullied before for not fitting in. They'd been arrested for their faith in Jesus Christ, had their businesses ransacked and their property stolen, and their kids had been beaten up on the way home from school.

And while we've already painted a pretty grim picture of these ancient believers' lives, there's one more bit of bad news. Things were going to get even worse, and Nero was to blame.

Any portrait of Christianity in the first century that doesn't include Nero isn't complete, because it's not bleak enough. Nero was the Darth Vader of early Christendom.

Remember the old saying about Nero fiddling while Rome burned? Well, it's not far from the truth. Nero was sliding south in the polls, so many historians think he was the mastermind behind the great fire that destroyed Rome in AD 64. Nero believed he could recapture the people's loyalty by riding in on a white horse after the tragedy and rebuilding the city to its former glory. But his plan backfired—no pun intended—and instead of returning to cheers, Nero rode back into Rome facing innuendos and jeers. Rumors circulated that he was to blame, that his soldiers started the blaze, and that the emperor had "fiddled" while their beloved city burned to the ground. So Nero desperately needed someone else to pin the blame on. He found the perfect scapegoat in those "intolerant, monotheistic, cannibalistic" Christians.[4]

The Hebrews had to learn how to stand firm in the face of persecution. And their first lesson was a tough one. Their teacher, the writer of Hebrews, made it clear that the days ahead would be more dangerous than anything they had walked through before.

> *In your struggle against sin you have not yet resisted to the point of shedding your blood.*
>
> Hebrews 12:4

Gulp. A bruised ego, black eye, or broken window is bearable. But bloodshed is something altogether different. The Hebrews didn't know martyrdom was part of the deal, and they weren't sure they could handle it.

Read Hebrews 13:22 and Acts 13:15. There is a phrase in both of these verses that is translated from the Greek word *parakaleō*, which is used in association with speaking, not writing. This causes many Bible scholars to believe that Hebrews was first spoken as a sermon. Are you prone to pay closer attention when listening to a dramatic sermon or reading a good book?

Read Hebrews 5:11; 6:9; and 11:32. List some of the reasons that the style of Hebrews seems to be sermonic. How might they affect the way you'll read it?

Have you been there? Have you ever gotten to the point of wanting to walk away from God because walking with Him is so hard? Or maybe you've pondered being a little less committed . . .

taking a few steps back from His demanding presence to the sure footing of mediocrity.

If you have, you're certainly not alone. From the beginning of history, God's people have found that following Him can be very difficult. Abraham decided God was taking too long to fulfill His audacious promise about his heirs outnumbering the stars, so he gave in to Sarah's Jerry Springer scheme for starting a family. Moses balked at the burning bush and stuttered in fear when God told him to go home and escort the Israelites out of Egypt. Elijah cried and uttered a halfhearted suicide threat—right after witnessing God's power and glory on Mount Carmel—when evil Queen Jezebel harassed him. And the disciples wilted, deserting Jesus when the Cross became reality instead of rhetoric. We all have a habit of retreating when the going gets tough.

> **More Info**
>
> Want to know more about the struggles Abraham, Moses, and Elijah faced? You can find Abraham's story in Genesis 16. The story of Moses is found in Exodus 3, and Elijah's tale is told in 1 Kings 19.

Devil in a Blue Dress

Several years ago I was invited to teach at a national Christian women's conference in Chattanooga. I was excited about the opportunity because I really liked the other women on the program and I had a lot of respect for the ministry sponsor. Little did I know that what was shaping up to be a wonderful weekend would also include verbal fisticuffs.

Almost everything went smoothly during the conference. The worship was engaging and Christ-centered, and the audience was gracious and attentive—except for this one woman in the front row who kept disrupting the program with loud comments, gestures, and strange gyrations that I assume were her idea of dancing before the Lord. Needless to say, our upfront dancer was very distracting, but we all tried to be polite and ignore her outbursts.

At the end of the day I was asked to facilitate a time of confession and commitment, which is one of my favorite things to do. It's incredible watching people's faces transform with the belief that God actually loves them and the relief that He's forgiven all the dark secrets from their past. Anyway, when the time of commitment ended and everyone began to leave the sanctuary, the gyrating woman from the front row approached me. I stepped toward her, thinking maybe she wanted to talk or pray. Instead, she leaned in too close for comfort and let me have it.

She angrily declared that God would never bless me as long as I dressed like a harlot, which was really confusing since I was wearing an ankle-length skirt, boots, a turtleneck, and a sweater. I could have understood her outrage if I was instructing in a tube top, but the only skin not covered was on my hands. And I've never been accused of having provocative wrists or fingers, so I'm not sure what was so offensive about my outfit! She went on to call me several more colorful names, then stopped abruptly, smiled, and walked away.

That day I really wanted to quit teaching altogether. Traveling to and from conferences thirty weekends a year is demanding enough; dealing with the one or two or ten oddballs who seem to infect such events is absolutely *exhausting*. I was tired of wearing a bull's-eye simply because I stood behind a podium. I didn't want to deal with the bruises that come from bumping up against others in the body of Christ anymore.

The life we're called to lead as followers of Christ can be very difficult. We're often faced with trouble from those who don't understand our faith. Rather than being appreciated for our commitment to godly behavior, we're criticized—even demonized by those who don't understand our faith—as being judgmental and narrow-minded. We're ridiculed for trusting in an invisible God. We're scorned for calling God "loving" while also believing He will condemn unrepentant sinners. And the difficult people we have to deal with aren't always *outside* our faith. Other Christians are sometimes odd and obnoxious; it can be embarrassing to even be associated with people the Bible defines as our close relatives.

People in Rome first thought Jews and Christians were synonymous, until the Jews let them know they didn't want to be associated with those "strange believers in Jesus Christ." Has someone ever assumed you believed in something you didn't or lumped you in with a religious group you disagreed with? How did you respond?

In light of all these issues, it's easy to see why most of us have pondered throwing in the proverbial towel at one time or another. Have you ever wondered about how good it would feel to sleep late on a Sunday, to cuss in traffic with no guilty conscience, to never be persecuted for your beliefs again?

It makes perfect sense that the frightened Hebrews, young in the faith, facing impossible odds, would also consider quitting.

 Read Isaiah 40:28-31. The "sermon" of Hebrews was given to a group of absolutely exhausted believers who epitomized weariness. When was the last time you were so spiritually exhausted that you didn't think you could go any further? How did God encourage you to keep going?

2

The Beginning
of the "Better Than's"

Read Hebrews 1

I learned to snowboard when I lived in Colorado,
and it quickly became one of my favorite sports.
Surfing down a mountain on a blanket of fresh
snow is exhilarating. I'm also fond of boarding
fashion. Unlike ski outfits, which tend to cut off my
circulation if I eat so much as half a bagel, my
snowboarding pants are baggy enough to make rap
stars jealous. The style is so voluminous, it's hard
to tell who's under all that Gore-Tex, which makes
for some very interesting encounters!

Last year when I was snowboarding, a young
man sidled up to me and initiated a conversation. I
answered his questions warmly, thinking how
unusual it was for a typically sullen teenager to be
so conversational. But when he edged closer and
smoothly offered to share his cigarette, it dawned
on me that he was flirting! I thought, *If this poor boy*

realized he was trying to hook up with a forty-year-old Bible teacher, he'd probably suffer irreparable psychological damage! It would have behooved him to find out a little information—like the fact that I was older than his mother—before he tried to bond over bad pick-up lines and nicotine.

In much the same way, if we want to understand the context of Hebrews, we need to find out more about the author. Of course, this presents a challenge because the writer is technically classified as anonymous. Scholars speculate on his identity, and arguments have been made for Barnabas, Aquila, Paul, and Luke.

My vote for authorship goes to Dr. Luke because the style of his Gospel account is very similar to Hebrews. Still, no one knows for certain who composed this book.

We do know some interesting things about him, though. He talks about Timothy, so he was at least acquainted with the apostolic circle. In light of his sophisticated use of Greek and his huge vocabulary, we can assume that he was well educated. He uses numerous Old Testament references—some obscure—so there's a good chance he was Jewish like his audience. Finally, he uses affectionate terms like "brothers" and "friends" and talks about shared experiences, so he knew the people he was writing to. And based on the warmth of his words, he knew them well.

I like the mental picture of Luke standing on a platform, using passionate gestures, stories, and inflection to inspire this group of fearful believers. And since I've always been partial to big, strong

FAST FACT

A popular hypothesis in feminist circles cites Aquila's wife, Priscilla, as the author of Hebrews. Although it might be politically correct to agree with assertive women everywhere, the text of Hebrews includes many masculine pronouns, so unless the writer had serious gender confusion issues, the Priscilla option isn't really valid.

men in tights bursting through paper signs, we're going to dramatize this pastor's personality with a football analogy.

Let's pretend it's halftime, and the Hebrew Titans are getting beat like a drum. The other team is playing dirty—biting and kicking— and the referees aren't making any calls against them because they've been bribed to look the other way. Plus the Hebrews are the visiting team, up against a huge home-field advantage. The fans aren't just heckling the Hebrews—they're throwing eggs and bottles. It feels more like a war zone than a football field. The team trudges into the locker room, bruised and bleeding, exhausted and discouraged. Trailing behind them is their beloved coach, who's determined to encourage his team to keep fighting, to hang in there, and to be faithful to the game plan in spite of the difficult circumstances.

And this is how the "coach" of Hebrews begins his halftime speech:

> *Long ago, at many times and in many ways, God spoke to our fathers by the prophets, but in these last days he has spoken to us by his Son, whom he appointed the heir of all things, through whom also he created the world. He is the radiance of the glory of God and the exact imprint of his nature, and he upholds the universe by the word of his power. After making purification for sins, he sat down at the right hand of the Majesty on high, having become as much superior to angels as the name he has inherited is more excellent than theirs.*

Hebrews 1:1-4

FAST FACT

Based on the references to spoken instead of written words in the book of Hebrews, several Old Testament academics believe it is the only New Testament book that was a sermon before it was recorded in textual form.[1] In other words, the "author" of Hebrews possibly could have been the pastor of this church.

Not your typical "Get back in the game!" speech, is it? However, if you'll just keep reading, I think you'll agree that this particular pep talk was *exactly* what our Hebrew friends needed to hear.

THE WORLD DWARFS US ALL, BUT GOD DWARFS THE WORLD. THE WORLD IS HIS FOOTSTOOL, ABOVE WHICH HE SITS SECURE. HE IS GREATER THAN THE WORLD AND ALL THAT IS IN IT, SO THAT ALL THE FEVERISH ACTIVITY OF ITS BUSTLING MILLIONS DOES NO MORE TO AFFECT HIM THAN THE CHIRPING AND JUMPING OF GRASSHOPPERS IN THE SUMMER SUN DOES TO AFFECT US. J. I. PACKER

When does the supreme position of our heavenly Father and Jesus the Son tend to make you feel small and insignificant . . . and when does His authority tend to make you feel secure and confident?

A Whiff of Greatness

One of the highlights of my preadolescent education happened when I was in the third grade. The entire elementary school gathered in the cafeteria to eat together, which brought delight or despair depending on what was in your lunch-box. On this particular day, I happened to be on the receiving end of the despair. Although my lunch usually consisted of something on whole wheat bread, on this occasion, my mother had finally given in to my desperate pleas for store-bought ravioli. Little did I know that pillows of pasta generously stuffed with

100 percent beef could smell so awful. The kids around me held their noses and quickly came up with a rhyming ditty about my malodorous lunch. Students at nearby tables soon joined in and encouraged more verses about smelly ravioli. There is no shame like being taunted by a choir of eight-year-old boys.

Suddenly, my tormentors stopped short. A group of very official-looking men had entered the dining hall. We all watched in reverent silence as Mr. Butler, our normally reserved principal, jumped up and strode energetically to greet the visitors. It was obvious the one with broad shoulders in blue pinstripes was the leader because the others flanked him with respectful deference and Mr. Butler shook his hand the hardest. My classmates gasped when this man walked through the rows of faded green Formica tables and headed straight toward me. Then, with surprising tenderness, he leaned down and said, "Hey, sweetheart, are you having a good day?"

His name was John Angel, he was the superintendent of schools, and he was my new stepfather. The indignity of stinky pasta faded away when he hugged me. I was a little embarrassed by the attention, but mostly I was proud. My stepdad was a big deal—even the principal acknowledged it—and I was somehow connected to his greatness.

The writer of Hebrews knew that a connection to someone of greatness would give his team a real feeling of power and advantage. So in the very first verses, he proclaims the superiority of Jesus, the fact that He is a much "bigger deal" than anyone or anything else. Although Jesus often hides His supremacy—choosing a stable and shepherds over a birthing suite and engraved announcements, and death on a cross over a military dictatorship—He is still the reigning King of kings and Lord of lords. Everyone else pales next to His power and glory. And His preeminence is such an important point that the pastor of Hebrews doesn't stop to take a breath while explaining it to his flock. Those first four verses (Hebrews 1:1-4)—comparing Jesus with the Old Covenant—are actually one superlong sentence!

 Read Hebrews 1:1-4. If Hebrews was written largely to encourage Christians wilting under persecution, why do you think the author starts with a "dissertation" on the supremacy of Christ?

Urim and Thummim
"holy dice" that priests threw in order to discern the will of God

Theophany
a visible manifestation of God's presence.

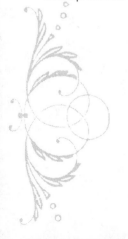

Better Than All the Rest
Several years ago, my friend Kim and her sister Lacey overheard their five-year-olds, Benjamin and Guston, comparing their culinary skills. The boys were eating a meal Lacey—Gus's mom—had cooked and it definitely was not canned pasta. She's a gifted chef, and while Kim is no slouch in the kitchen, her lifestyle involves a lot of travel, so she's a familiar customer at some of Nashville's better takeout restaurants. Therefore, when Gus looked over at his cousin and happily announced, "My mom makes the best food ever," Lacey winced inwardly and wondered how Benji was going to respond. He paused for a few seconds and then

retorted, "Well, my mom knows where to *get* the best food ever!"

Comparisons are risky in human relationships, but the author of Hebrews knew they were imperative in order to give his team the proper perspective. He wanted his players to understand that nothing could ever measure up to Jesus—that He's better than *everything*.

The verses we just read reveal the superiority of Jesus over the Old Revelation, otherwise known as the Old Testament. In the old revelation, God spoke "at many times and in many ways." He used the written Word, the Urim and Thummim, theophanies, visions, dreams, signs, and prophets.

But we don't have to translate from flaming topiaries or search for signs in the sky anymore because God relates to us through His Son. And Jesus is a direct line to God. He's a perfectly clear—no ogling dice, squinting at hedges, or interpreting dreams— liaison. Thus, Jesus is *better than* the old religious system.

> **More Info**
>
> Want to know more? To learn about one of God's most famous theophanies, read Exodus 3, the story of Moses and the burning bush.

Higher Than the Angels

As he expounds on Jesus' greatness, the writer of Hebrews continues with the comparison, this time showing Jesus in connection with the angels:

> *For to which of the angels did God ever say, "You are my Son, today I have begotten you"? Or again, "I will be to him a father, and he shall be to me a son"?* Hebrews 1:5

Notice that the language in Hebrews 1:5 isn't a statement; it's a question, underscoring the truth that God didn't call the angels His "Son." This verse highlights the unique relationship between God the Father and Jesus the Son. If someone handed our Creator a camera, He'd surely focus on Jesus because Jesus is His beloved offspring! Even His name is superior to angels—"Son" as opposed to "messenger." Jesus receives worship, while the angels give worship. Jesus sits enthroned at God's right hand, while angels serve God and man. Angels are awesome, but Jesus is much better!

Read Hebrews 1:4-14. Compare and contrast Jesus' position with that of angels. Share at least three differences.

 While Hebrews makes it clear that Jesus is superior to angels, it's also clear that angels are messengers from God, "sent to serve those who will inherit salvation" (1:14, NIV). Although Hollywood and the psychic network have propagated cartoonish, unbiblical examples of angels, they do exist. God created them for His glory and our good. Explain how you think angels might "serve" believers. Share specific personal examples, if possible.

The Liability of the Law
The final matchup made in the first chapter of Hebrews pits Jesus against Old Testament Law. I don't think anyone except a religious Jew could comprehend the seeming audacity of this compari-

son. The Law was sacred above all else in Jewish culture. Only a few select men (scribes, rabbis, etc.) were allowed to study and discuss it. Everyone else just labored to remember and obey every tiny detail they'd been taught about the Law so as to stay on God's good side.

The Law was the only measuring stick Jews had

Did you know?

Interestingly, philosophers and pagan priests during the first century attempted to manipulate Hebrews 1:5 to promote the heresy of dualism. Dualism proposed that the physical world (whatever you can touch, taste, see, or feel) was unholy, while anything intangible was of higher spiritual value. Proponents argued that angels were closer to God and beat Jesus on the supernatural scoreboard because they didn't inhabit a human body. Plus, they reasoned, angels didn't sully themselves by cavorting with really dirty people like lepers, prostitutes, and tax collectors the way Jesus had.

Some Jewish Christian converts were tempted to believe this pseudo-academic hogwash because angels had always been very significant in their religious history. For instance, when Moses gave the final blessing to Israel before his death, he began by reminiscing about the angels who appeared with God on Mount Sinai:

The LORD came from Sinai and dawned from Seir upon us; he shone forth from Mount Paran; he came from the ten thousands of holy ones, with flaming fire at his right hand.

Deuteronomy 33:2

Remember, Mount Sinai was the place God gave Moses the law (the Ten Commandments) on stone tablets—first inscribed with His own fingers, then engraved by Moses after he got mad at the Israelites' irreverent party and shattered the first set (for the unabridged version of this story, see Exodus 19–34). And the fact that "ten thousands of holy ones" were with Jehovah on this momentous occasion put angels on a pedestal in Jewish doctrine.[2]

to evaluate their relationship with God. The only way they knew to please Him was through strict adherence to His rules. And, just like us, the Hebrew converts—who had experienced the grace of the gospel—often fell back into the habit of keeping track of their own righteousness.

Read Psalm 45:6-7 and Hebrews 1:8-9. Why do you think the writer of Hebrews quotes from this "wedding" Psalm when referring to the superiority of Jesus? How does the hope we have in Christ compare to a royal wedding?

So imagine the looks of surprise, relief, and

did you know?

The following excerpt is from the Mishnah (a collection of oral laws, codified in the second century, which form a basic part of the Talmud, or Jewish law)[3] dealing with the subject of resting on the Sabbath.

The main classes of work are forty save one: sowing, ploughing, reaping, binding sheaves, threshing, winnowing, cleansing crops, grinding, sifting, kneading, baking, shearing wool, washing or beating or dyeing it, spinning, weaving, making two loops, weaving two threads, separating two threads, tying a knot, loosening a knot, sewing two stitches, tearing in order to sew two stitches, hunting a gazelle, slaughtering or flaying or salting it or curing its skin, scraping it or cutting it up, writing two letters, erasing in order to write two letters, building, pulling down, putting out a fire, lighting a fire, striking with a hammer and taking out aught from one domain to another.[4]

Of course, more recent rabbinic writings have updated some of the items listed since few people struggle with the whole gazelle issue today. But this selection helps elucidate the kind of legalistic minutiae Jews were bound by.

perhaps even conviction when their pastor quoted from Psalm 45 to remind his listeners that even the Law holds the throne of Jesus above everything else:

> *But of the Son he says, "Your throne, O God,*
> *is forever and ever, the scepter of uprightness is*
> *the scepter of your kingdom. You have loved*
> *righteousness and hated wickedness; therefore*
> *God, your God, has anointed you with the oil*
> *of gladness beyond your companions."*
>
> Hebrews 1:8-9

Those words must have sounded like a "Get Out of Jail Free" card to the Hebrews. After experiencing the religious tyranny enforced by joyless Pharisees, their tender shepherd reminds them it's the posture of their heart—not the style of their clothing, the length of their hair, or whether or not they hunted gazelles on the Sabbath—that matters to God. Observing sacred rules apart from a relationship with the Messiah is futile!

Paul elaborated on this point in his letter to the Christians in Galatia (now modern Turkey):

> *Is the law then contrary to the promises of God?*
> *Certainly not! For if a law had been given that*
> *could give life, then righteousness would indeed be*
> *by the law. But the Scripture imprisoned every-*
> *thing under sin, so that the promise by faith in*
> *Jesus Christ might be given to those who believe.*
>
> *Now before faith came, we were held captive*
> *under the law, imprisoned until the coming faith*
> *would be revealed. So then, the law was our*

*guardian until Christ came, in order that we might
be justified by faith. But now that faith has come,
we are no longer under a guardian, for in Christ
Jesus you are all sons of God, through faith.*

Galatians 3:21-26

God's law is good—it's His supernatural instruction book and love letter to us—but it has limits. It can define sin, but it can't redeem us from sin. Once again, Jesus is *better than* the law.

Strangers in a Strange Land

The Hebrews obviously didn't fit in Greco-Roman culture and were persecuted as a result. In what ways does your love for God cause you to feel like you don't fit in your hometown? Have you ever felt persecuted for your faith? If so, how?

I once dated a nuclear physicist, and as you can probably imagine, we were poster children for the "opposites attract" school of thought. He liked playing chess; I prefer charades. He liked complex mathematical problems; I'd like someone else to balance my checkbook. He talked slowly and deliberately; I fell asleep during some of our phone conversations. But he was a really nice Christian guy, and I thought it would be interesting to go out with a man who read something besides *Sports Illustrated*.

I visited him one weekend when he was completing his postdoctoral fellowship at Harvard (just

writing those words makes me feel intellectual by association), and we decided to drive out to Cape Cod since neither of us had been to that part of New England before. We made reservations at a hotel—separate quarters, of course—on the very tip of the Cape, loaded bikes on the roof of his car, and drove out of Boston with what seemed like half the city's population.

After we checked in, we got on our bikes and started exploring. The path was hilly, dotted with historic lighthouses and beautiful views of the ocean. We peddled for hours, enjoying the scenery and solitude. When our stomachs started rumbling, we headed back toward town to get something to eat. As we got closer to civilization, I noticed that men seemed to be staring at us. At first I thought they were looking at me, so I held in my stomach and smiled. But soon I realized they were admiring my boyfriend in his biking shorts! Although it occurred to me that I hadn't seen any women or children since we'd arrived, I still didn't quite understand what was going on. It took a little more time, and one embarrassing restaurant incident, before we both figured out that we'd unwittingly stumbled upon a town that catered to homosexual men.

I'll never forget walking into a little café and having the proprietor greet my beau warmly, only to give us both the cold shoulder when he discovered we were a couple. I was hoping for a muffin and some coffee instead of condemnation. That catastrophe in Massachusetts is one of the few times I've ever been treated like a pariah.

But Jewish Christians were reviled constantly. Not only were they ignored at the neighborhood coffee shop, they were being killed because of what they believed. Therefore, the temptation to turn back—to renounce Jesus and revert back to Judaism—was strong. As practicing Jews, they'd be tolerated by Greco-Roman culture. They could still worship God the *Father* and have the nostalgic consolation of ritual; they just wouldn't claim the Jesus-as-Messiah part.

The coach of this battle-weary team of believers knew the discouragement his team was facing. He understood the price they were paying for worshipping Jesus Christ, Son of God. This is why he begins his exhortation by extolling Jesus' superiority to the old revelation, angels, and the Law. He wants his team to remember that a *relationship* with Jesus is far better than the religion of their youth.

Commentator Warren Wiersbe writes that Hebrews is a book of examination. What obstacles tend to keep you from really examining your intimacy—or lack thereof—with God?

3

Drifting Away Again

Read Hebrews 2

I grew up in central Florida, where boats are as common as kudzu in Atlanta, and bass fishing is considered the sport of kings. Consequently, I "wasted" hundreds of childhood hours sitting on a sweaty plastic seat cushion watching mosquitoes swarm over the brown surface of Lake Monroe, while my lure attracted nothing but water lilies. I've never been able to muster up the passion for casting a line that my brother and stepfather have, but I do like the atmosphere surrounding the whole fishing experience.

Boat docks are wonderful microcosms of sights and smells, where men are separated from boys by the size of their motors. It's fascinating to watch some of them strut around, especially those who don't appear to be the least bit outdoorsy or athletic yet still pull into the parking lot dragging a boat behind the family sedan. They're usually the ones with white legs and black socks, smeared with sunscreen—their arms full of poles, life jackets, bug repellant, and a big cooler. It's as if the purchase of a dinghy has catapulted them from anonymous bean counter to confident, courageous captain of the high seas!

I remember one such man trying to maneuver his boat down to the water. My stepdad and others quickly offered to help because this man's lack of experience with a trailer was fairly obvious. But he declined their assistance with a jaunty wave, so we all sat back to watch and wait (only one boat at a time could use the ramp at this particular lake). It took several attempts for him to back up the boat correctly, and when he finally did, he jumped out of his car triumphantly. But in his haste to prove his fishermanliness, the man forgot to put his car in park. His overconfidence quickly turned to dismay as his Honda rolled backward into the lake and was soon buried beneath the waves.

 "Spiritual drifting" refers to behavior that's not overtly corrupt yet still diverts our attention from God. What are the biggest distractions in your life right now?

The Danger of Drifting

Our Hebrews pastor uses the first of several nautical references in chapter 2 when he warns these young believers about neglecting their salvation:

> *Therefore we must pay much closer attention to what we have heard, lest we drift away from it.*

For since the message declared by angels proved to
be reliable and every transgression or disobedience
received a just retribution, how shall we escape if
we neglect such a great salvation? It was declared
at first by the Lord, and it was attested to us
by those who heard, while God also bore witness
by signs and wonders and various miracles and by
gifts of the Holy Spirit distributed according
to his will. Hebrews 2:1-4

To "drift away" was the kind of language often used at that time to describe a ship that had been allowed to float past the harbor.[1] And the "message declared by angels" is referring to the gospel. The author is trying to explain to the Hebrews that their lives will be ruined—metaphorically *shipwrecked*—if they drift from the faith they have in Christ.

The writer of Hebrews is using such dramatic imagery in order to grab these disheartened Hebrews by the shoulders and shake some sense into them. He wants them to understand that no matter what difficulties they may face in the future, the consequence of forsaking Jesus would be far worse. Without Christ, their lives would be worthless flotsam or like some soggy car dredged from the bottom of a lake.

Interestingly, the process of spiritual drifting isn't usually dramatic at all. Prodigal seasons are rarely launched with spectacular, well-thought-out strategies. They typically begin with just one minor moment of rebellion—a slight exaggeration on a tax return, a little off-color late-night TV, a flirtatious glance at someone else's spouse.

If you aren't paying attention, you might not even notice that you've started to drift until you're a very long way from where you started.

In what ways do you think the lines between Christian values and cultural traditions have become blurred? How does that make spiritual drifting a greater possibility?

One Small Step for Mankind

One of the most powerful speakers I've ever heard is a woman named Iris Urrey (now Iris Urrey Blue). I've never met her personally, and I only heard her speak one time, at a summer camp when I was eighteen years old. But I've never forgotten what she said—or how she said it.

She talked about growing up in a loving home with Christian values, but she still struggled with insecurity because she was so much taller than other kids her age. Her insecurity prompted her to make some really dumb decisions. She told us how she snuck out to go to a bar with some friends when she was just thirteen. Because of her height, everyone—including men in the bar that night—thought she was much older. One handsome stranger asked her to dance. She'd never even been out with a boy before, much less danced with a man.

He was also the first man to tell Iris she was beautiful, and before she really knew what was happening, he had charmed her into spending the night with him. Too ashamed to go back home after the experience, she moved into his apartment. Soon she was doing favors for him far worse than anything she had ever imagined.

While most of her friends were going to ball
games and whispering about their dream prom
date, she was walking the streets as a prostitute.
Then she began using narcotics to numb the
emotional pain. In order to finance her drug habit,
she decided to rob a convenience store. She told us
how her size made her a conspicuous thief. "I was
so tall, I might as well have looked right into that
little video camera and said, 'Hi, my name's Iris,'"
she said. She was eventually convicted for armed
robbery and sent to prison.

Iris Urrey's story kept five hundred summer
campers spellbound. I don't think any of us had
ever heard such a colorful testimony, especially not
from a really tall redhead with a big Texas accent.
We were stunned to hear how her journey of
self-destruction began with one forbidden dance.
One small step of disobedience had led to years of
sorrow. Over and over again Iris emphasized that
"one sin always leads to another." The story of how
God redeemed the wreckage of her life was incredible. But her dramatic warning about drifting still
rings loudest in my heart.

Have you drifted from the sweet intimacy that
once defined your relationship with God?

**Read Psalm 121. What does God promise about
us slipping from our secure place in Him?**

An Empathetic Hero

Just when the sermon gets a little too close for
comfort and we're all cringing from the memory of
our own personal drifting pattern, the writer of

Hebrews sends up a flare of hope. We're reminded that Jesus Himself knows what it's like to be human.

> *For it was fitting that he, for whom and by whom all things exist, in bringing many sons to glory, should make the founder of their salvation perfect through suffering. For he who sanctifies and those who are sanctified all have one origin. That is why he is not ashamed to call them brothers, saying, "I will tell of your name to my brothers; in the midst of the congregation I will sing your praise."*
> *And again, "I will put my trust in him." And again, "Behold, I and the children God has given me."*
>
> *Since therefore the children share in flesh and blood, he himself likewise partook of the same things, that through death he might destroy the one who has the power of death, that is, the devil, and deliver all those who through fear of death were subject to lifelong slavery. For surely it is not angels that he helps, but he helps the offspring of Abraham. Therefore he had to be made like his brothers in every respect, so that he might become a merciful and faithful high priest in the service of God, to make propitiation for the sins of the people.*
> *For because he himself has suffered when tempted, he is able to help those who are being tempted.*
>
> Hebrews 2:10-18

When I was on staff at a church in Nashville, the computer system was one of the few things that tempted me to use bad words in the workplace. At least once a month, we had some technical glitch that would cause everyone's computer to revolt. Then we'd have to dig out pens and paper and vainly attempt to recall the information in the critical—but now deleted—file we had just been working on.

Our productivity was all but paralyzed until the computer consultant arrived on the scene. He usually walked in several nail-biting hours later, talking to another obviously desperate client on one of his cell phones (he carried two, along with a beeper). His gadgets alone made him seem like some kind of mainframe superhero striding in to save the day.

Public speaking is part of my job. I've had the privilege of standing before audiences with as many as twenty thousand people—but I couldn't string two intelligent words together when trying to explain my computer woes to this expert. I felt like the proverbial woman who makes car noises for a bemused mechanic because she doesn't know the correct automotive jargon.

And attempting to understand the consultant's language was even more humiliating. He used a words-combined-with-numbers dialect I'd never heard before. So I typically just stood there, grunting and gesturing, feeling like a complete idiot. I could tell he thought I was dumb, too, because the longer he was in my office, the slower he spoke. I still get a little nervous walking past the computer department when I'm innocently browsing for something else in an electronics store. I'm afraid red lights will start flashing and computer experts will come running from all directions screaming, "Step away from the equipment, lady! Step away!"

Jesus is a very different kind of champion. He certainly qualifies as a genius—*the* expert on every subject—but He doesn't patronize us. Instead of rolling His eyes and snickering at our mistakes, He mercifully claims us as family. Even though our Savior is familiar with every crack in the foundation of our commitment, every doubt, every fear, every temptation to turn from the truth, He still calls us kin.

> *Since the One who saves and those who are saved have a common origin, Jesus doesn't hesitate to treat them as family, saying,*
>
> > *I'll tell my good friends, my brothers and*
> > *sisters, all I know about you;*
> > *I'll join them in worship and praise*
> > *to you.*
>
> Hebrews 2:11-12 (The Message)

Only the Christian God, the Messiah, condescended from heaven to earth, from supernatural being to bawling infant. Rather than demanding that we aspire to godhood in order to be in relationship with Him, He left God's side to be with us. He walked and talked and laughed and bled and dwelt among us. He chose to share in our frail humanity so that He could redeem us from it. He wore a suit of skin so that we could be free from the fear of death and really live.

Bᴜᴛ ꜱᴜᴘᴘᴏꜱɪɴɢ Gᴏᴅ ʙᴇᴄᴀᴍᴇ ᴀ ᴍᴀɴ—ꜱᴜᴘᴘᴏꜱᴇ
ᴏᴜʀ ʜᴜᴍᴀɴ ɴᴀᴛᴜʀᴇ ᴡʜɪᴄʜ ᴄᴀɴ ꜱᴜꜰꜰᴇʀ ᴀɴᴅ ᴅɪᴇ
ᴡᴀꜱ ᴀᴍᴀʟɢᴀᴍᴀᴛᴇᴅ ᴡɪᴛʜ Gᴏᴅ'ꜱ ɴᴀᴛᴜʀᴇ ɪɴ ᴏɴᴇ
ᴘᴇʀꜱᴏɴ—ᴛʜᴇɴ ᴛʜᴀᴛ ᴘᴇʀꜱᴏɴ ᴄᴏᴜʟᴅ ʜᴇʟᴘ ᴜꜱ. Hᴇ
ᴄᴏᴜʟᴅ ꜱᴜʀʀᴇɴᴅᴇʀ Hɪꜱ ᴡɪʟʟ, ᴀɴᴅ ꜱᴜꜰꜰᴇʀ ᴀɴᴅ
ᴅɪᴇ, ʙᴇᴄᴀᴜꜱᴇ Hᴇ ᴡᴀꜱ ᴍᴀɴ; ᴀɴᴅ Hᴇ ᴄᴏᴜʟᴅ ᴅᴏ ɪᴛ
ᴘᴇʀꜰᴇᴄᴛʟʏ ʙᴇᴄᴀᴜꜱᴇ Hᴇ ᴡᴀꜱ Gᴏᴅ ... Bᴜᴛ ᴡᴇ
ᴄᴀɴɴᴏᴛ ꜱʜᴀʀᴇ Gᴏᴅ'ꜱ ᴅʏɪɴɢ ᴜɴʟᴇꜱꜱ Gᴏᴅ ᴅɪᴇꜱ; ᴀɴᴅ
Hᴇ ᴄᴀɴɴᴏᴛ ᴅɪᴇ ᴇxᴄᴇᴘᴛ ʙʏ ʙᴇɪɴɢ ᴀ ᴍᴀɴ. Tʜᴀᴛ ɪꜱ
ᴛʜᴇ ꜱᴇɴꜱᴇ ɪɴ ᴡʜɪᴄʜ Hᴇ ᴘᴀʏꜱ ᴏᴜʀ ᴅᴇʙᴛ, ᴀɴᴅ
ꜱᴜꜰꜰᴇʀꜱ ꜰᴏʀ ᴜꜱ ᴡʜᴀᴛ Hᴇ Hɪᴍꜱᴇʟꜰ ɴᴇᴇᴅ ɴᴏᴛ
ꜱᴜꜰꜰᴇʀ ᴀᴛ ᴀʟʟ.[2]   C. S. LEWIS

Hallelujah, what a hero!

Radiant Results

There's a sober verse in the passage on page 32
(Hebrews 2:10-18) that merits further scrutiny
before we sail on to chapter 3:

> *For it was fitting that he, for whom and by whom*
> *all things exist, in bringing many sons to glory,*
> *should make the founder of their salvation perfect*
> *through suffering.*   Hebrews 2:10

At first glance, this verse reads as if Jesus wasn't
perfect until He suffered, but that's not the case.
Jesus is perfect—past, present, and future. The
English words "make perfect" in this verse are a bit
misleading. They come from one Greek word,
teleioō, which can be translated "to complete, to
finish, to reach a goal, or to be fulfilled."[3] It's the
same word used to describe when a Jewish high
priest was consecrated for service. Jesus wasn't

"made perfect" through suffering; He was *preparing* to reach the goal of our redemption. He felt our pain in order to lead us out of it.

Read Hebrews 2:11-13; Matthew 28:10; and John 20:17. Jesus didn't directly refer to His disciples—or us—as "brothers" or "family" until *after* His resurrection. Why not?

Do you ever wonder why, since our merciful Redeemer allowed Himself to be made ready for the Cross through pain, we try to avoid it at all costs? Most of us do everything we can to sidestep the slightest twinge of discomfort. We insulate ourselves with work, superficial relationships, and lukewarm religion. In our quest to reduce the risk of heartache, we lock ourselves into prisons of artifice. Have you ever heard someone quote Romans 8:28—God will work all this out for good!—prematurely and with complete inappropriateness after a tragedy? I guess it's easier to spout a verse out of context rather than weep with someone who is grieving.

> **More Info**
>
> Want to know what the Bible says about how we should respond to someone who's hurting? Check out Romans 12:12-16.

Unlike Ted Danson's utopian bar, Cheers, where everyone knows your name, no one really knows us. We've memorized—maybe even cross-stitched—the verse about Christ's promise to give us life more abundantly (John 10:10), but the only things most of us experience in abundance are loneliness and disappointment. Dodging emotional pain makes for a depressing existence.

Read Hebrews 2:18 and 2 Corinthians 1:3-4. Describe an occasion when God allowed you to use a painful experience to help someone else walking through a similar situation.

The most joyful people I know are those who have experienced real sorrow. Several years ago I was teaching at a retreat where an absolutely radiant woman sat in the front row. I was so intrigued by the contentment and joy of her expression—she was practically luminescent—that I asked her to meet me for coffee after the program. After a few minutes of small talk, I told her that I'd never met someone who "glowed" quite like her. In response, she told me her story.

She had married young and married badly. Her husband was abusive, and after suffering for years, she finally found the courage to leave him. She was determined to protect her three children from his violent behavior. During their separation, he had visitation rights, and one weekend he decided to take their two boys camping. She felt uneasy about the trip but had no choice but to let them go. Her estranged husband then took those precious little boys into the woods and killed them before turning the gun on himself.

Her words left me speechless. With tears rolling down her face, she went on to talk about God's goodness in the midst of unbelievable sadness. She shared details of His compassion: how her sons didn't suffer, how her youngest had been spared because she insisted he was too young to go, how God had lifted her head when she could barely get out of bed. She talked about meeting and falling in love with her new husband—a godly, kind man—and having another child. When she explained how tragedy taught her that this world isn't our home, that she doesn't place her hope here the way she once did, and that she considers every day a gift from God's hand, I knew she meant what she said.

Sorrow had rubbed a patina on her soul that was visible on her face. I realized after our encounter that what I was drawn to was her clear reflection of Christ. Like Jesus, her beauty had been shaped through suffering.

Read Romans 8:18-25; 1 Peter 2:20-21; 5:1-2; and Philippians 1:29-30. Suffering isn't just a recurrent theme in Hebrews, it's woven throughout the whole Bible. What do these passages say about the reason we hurt?

> *For we know that the whole creation has been groaning together in the pains of childbirth until now. And not only the creation, but we ourselves, who have the firstfruits of the Spirit, groan inwardly as we wait eagerly for adoption as sons, the redemption of our bodies. For in this hope we were saved. Now hope that is seen is not hope. For who hopes for what he sees? But if we hope for what we do not see, we wait for it with patience.*
>
> Romans 8:22-25

DVD **Read Psalm 30:10-12. Describe how God has turned a time of grieving into a waltz in your life. How has suffering made you "sweeter"?**

What Are You Lookin' At?

Believe it or not, the most embarrassing moment I ever had at the beach didn't involve a bathing suit. I was in high school, and my friend Julie and I were resting our elbows on a float, kicking our legs underwater, just chatting away. We weren't paying attention to where the waves were taking us; we were just looking at each other while we talked. We floated for a long time until we heard sirens.

We turned the raft toward the beach to see what was happening and saw several emergency vehicles and an ambulance. Of course, we were so far from shore they looked like toy trucks. Then we saw two lifeguards dive into the water with torpedo buoys. Julie said, "Oh wow, somebody's getting rescued!" We watched them swim for a while before we realized there weren't any swimmers around us. They were racing through the water to rescue Julie and me!

We'd been so busy talking that we cruised right into rip currents. We didn't even notice the shark fin nearby that prompted the 911 call. We had been focused only on what was right in front of our faces. That is, until we were plopped on the sand— in front of our friends and potential boyfriends—by those courageous lifeguards!

Read Psalm 51:2. Would you define your relationship with Christ as thriving, limping along, or stagnant? How far have you floated from the intimacy you had at the beginning of your walk with Him? Do you need Him to restore the joy you once had?

The Hebrews also seemed oblivious to the spiritual danger they were floating toward. They were preoccupied with the things right in front of their eyes: brutal dictators, prison cells, and funerals for their friends. But their leader reminds them to stop drifting and to begin to pay close attention to what's really important: looking beyond their current circumstances, past the political harassment and barren cupboards, to the heroics of Jesus, their empathetic Hero.

> *Oh that you had paid attention to my command-ments! Then your peace would have been like a river.* Isaiah 48:18

4

People Don't Deserve Pedestals

Read Hebrews 3

It often gets so hot and humid in Nashville, you can see steam rising up off the asphalt. One weekend, I foolishly decided to get some exercise in the middle of the afternoon—reasoning that biking in the heat would burn more calories and help me sweat off a dress size or two. I poured myself into stretchy black biking shorts, for a streamlined sausage look, and started pedaling. Within minutes I was soaked in sweat, in an exercise-induced "zone"—legs pumping, mouth agape, eyes fixated on passing scenery. I rode past a country club pool, and soon all I could think about was water. The Caribbean-blue waves of Florida's Gulf Coast. A pristine mountain stream. Crashing waterfalls. Ponds. Electric tabletop fountains from Sharper Image.

After a cool shower, I started thinking about the

way my mind had become obsessed with water—
how seeing just one swimming pool had triggered
a series of aquamarine associations. I'll bet that
happened to the Hebrews, too. When their pastor
started talking about the heroics of Jesus, they
probably started thinking about other heroes. And
their musings would certainly have included
Moses, because along with Abraham and David,
Moses is one of the greatest heroes of Jewish
history.

Moses was a leader of epic proportions. I've had
the privilege of visiting Israel twice, and it seemed
that everywhere we went, we met men and boys
named Moses. You didn't hear any moms yelling
for Abednego or Zadok to come home for dinner,
but you did hear parents calling mini-Moseses. One
of our tour guides even answered to the name
Motie, which I soon found out was a common nick-
name for Moses.

**Read Hebrews 2:17–3:6. Most Bible scholars
think chapter 3 really should begin at 2:17.
Why do you think that is? What's the author
referring to when he starts with "Therefore" in
Hebrews 3:1?**

I think the Hebrews' pastor knew that the
subject of Christ's heroism would cause his congregation to daydream about Moses so he brings up
the subject:

> *Therefore, holy brothers, you who share in a heav-
> enly calling, consider Jesus, the apostle and high
> priest of our confession, who was faithful to him*

*who appointed him, just as Moses also was faithful
in all God's house. For Jesus has been counted
worthy of more glory than Moses—as much more
glory as the builder of a house has more honor than
the house itself. (For every house is built by someone, but the builder of all things is God.) Now
Moses was faithful in all God's house as a servant,
to testify to the things that were to be spoken later,
but Christ is faithful over God's house as a son.
And we are his house if indeed we hold fast our
confidence and our boasting in our hope.*

Hebrews 3:1-6

Silk Purses and Pig Ears

Most of us would love to be as highly regarded as
Moses. We tend to court the approval of others,
tipping more than usual when we're out with
friends, opening the door for an elderly woman at
the grocery store, letting a speeding stranger
merge into our lane—hoping our exemplary
behavior will be noticed and applauded. I think this
is because other people's praise often lessens our
own feelings of insecurity and insignificance.

I experienced someone's unusual, unmerited
approval a few years ago when I was speaking at a
conference and had been escorted to one of the back
rooms during the break. When I realized the
program was starting again, I began to work my
way down a dark corridor toward the stage door.
As I did so, I ran into another woman.

She was wearing a dirty T-shirt and looked a
little disheveled. She seemed flustered when we
first came face-to-face, but then she stepped

forward and asked if she could hug me. Her request startled me for a second. I'm not used to rumpled strangers asking for an embrace. But after a slight pause I said, "Of course you can hug me!" and tried to squeeze her with as much grace as I could muster.

But I sure wasn't prepared for her response. She moaned and then collapsed to the floor, quivering. I frantically looked around for a phone to call 911 because I thought she was having a seizure. Then she began to mutter as she was flailing about. I don't remember her exact words, but they had something to do with how "holy" I was and how blessed she was to be near me. This sweet, delusional woman thought she had been zapped by the Holy Spirit when she touched me. Was she ever mistaken! I didn't earn her favor, and I wasn't being the least bit holy at the time—I was wondering where my Barney Fife of a security officer was when I needed him!

To me, "Christian celebrity" seems as oxymoronic as jumbo shrimp. Just because someone can sing or teach or write books doesn't mean he or she is worthy of exaltation. And marketable gifts don't always represent Christian maturity. Some people have huge talent but tiny humility. Frankly, idolizing fellow believers is contrary to the gospel; it's like someone who's dying of thirst being enchanted with the plastic container rather than the life-giving water inside it!

The minute Peter came through the door, Cornelius was up on his feet greeting him—and then down on his face worshiping him! Peter

*pulled him up and said, "None of that—I'm a man
and only a man, no different from you."*
Acts 10:25-26 (*The Message*)

**Have you ever seen someone bow or grovel
before a prominent person the way Cornelius
did with Peter in Acts 10:25-26? How did it
make you feel?**

The pastor of Hebrews makes the same point as
Peter regarding the foolishness of human idoliza-
tion: We aren't worthy of being worshipped. Only
the Messiah is.

Respect versus Real Heroics

Although you may not be tempted to accost
strangers in church hallways, you still need to be
aware of who's on your pedestal. Because idolatry
often masquerades as spirituality.

When our church celebrates Reformation
Sunday in the fall, Martin Luther is the man of the
hour. Mr. Luther initiated the Protestant Reformation, lobbied for the poor, and risked his life for the
sake of the gospel. Hundreds of books have been
written about him, and denominations have been
named in his honor. His Bible commentaries and
other writings are still considered by many to be
the finest in Christian theory and literature. He
was a great man, but he also made big mistakes.

Several years into the reformation, Martin Luther
argued with a Swiss theologian named Zwingli,
who was also an enigmatic evangelical. Their argument involved the specific doctrine and nature of

Communion. Luther held to a more Catholic understanding of the sacraments. He was so furious about Zwingli's insistence that the observance of Communion was symbolic that he uttered these infamous words: "I'd rather drink blood with the papists than mere juice with the Zwinglians!"[1]

Martin Luther was a powerful tool in the hand of God, but he also opened up a painful rift with another Christian leader, a dispute that surely brought more harm than good to the cause of Christ. Like all men, Luther was prone to error. When you filter the mind of God through the vessel of man—regardless of which man or woman—it will always be distorted at some level.

Roy Carter is a good friend and one of my favorite Bible teachers. He graduated from an academically demanding seminary with honors and continues to study diligently and read voraciously. I've walked into his office many times to ask him about a confusing passage or how to pronounce some Hebrew or Greek word. He's one of the smartest pastors I know, and the wisest thing I've ever heard him say when he's preaching is this: "I'm probably teaching something wrong here, but I don't know what it is yet. I'll let you know as soon as I find out!"

We can't forget that along with men like Moses and Martin Luther, God used donkeys and rocks as messengers, too.

Rewrite the phrase "People don't deserve pedestals" in your own words. Can you find any Scripture to substantiate it?

Fifteen Minutes Too Long

I need a hero
I'm holding out for a hero 'til the end of the night
He's gotta be strong
And he's gotta be fast
And he's gotta be fresh from the fight
I need a hero
I'm holding out for a hero 'til the morning light
He's gotta be sure
And it's gotta be soon
And he's gotta be larger than life

Though flawed, at least Martin Luther *was* a messenger of the gospel—and the acclaim he received was largely for positive attributes like humility and integrity. Some modern-day heroes are praised solely for appearance and performance; morality seems to be irrelevant.

Little girls today look up to teenagers not much older than themselves, celebrities who wear dental floss disguised as fashion and brag about their sexual escapades. Boys admire professional athletes, some of whom are more famous for their off-color, off-the-field antics than for touchdowns scored or assists earned. Both boys and girls admire musical artists—and I use that term loosely because some I've heard can't even carry a tune or play an instrument—who sing shockingly explicit lyrics, have decided crotch-grabbing is an acceptable dance style, and wear felony convictions as badges of honor. I think their fifteen minutes of fame is about fourteen minutes and fifty-nine seconds too long.

I'm thankful the ban on bare legs in church has

been lifted (I think pantyhose were invented by a mean-spirited misogynist), and I'm glad crushed velvet paintings of Elvis are a thing of the past. But I wish behaving yourself in the limelight was still popular. It seems hooligans with publicists are the most likely to be called heroes in our culture. Noted historian and Pulitzer prize–winning author Daniel J. Boorstin lamented this sad phenomenon in a recent interview: "Celebrity-worship and hero-worship should not be confused. Yet we confuse them every day, and by doing so we come dangerously close to depriving ourselves of all real models. We lose sight of the men and women who do not seem great because they are famous but are famous because they are great. We come closer and closer to degrading all fame into notoriety."[2]

 Read Daniel Boorstin's quote again. What do you think the biggest difference should be between celebrity-worship and hero-worship?

Even the morally ambiguous *People* magazine explored a dangerous aspect of celebrity worship in a recent article about young girls trying to emulate the too-thin bodies of idols like Mary-Kate Olsen. Current media darling Jessica Simpson talked about the unrealistic images: "When I was younger, I tried to be skinny. There is so much pressure in today's society to look like the girl on the cover of the magazine. But [those photos] are airbrushed and have special lighting. She's gone through two hours of hair and makeup. That just sets expectations really high for young girls."

In this same article, Dr. Lawrence Bass, a

surgeon in New York, discussed the problem of teens requesting plastic surgery and the inherent risks of such procedures. "Their bodies are not done transforming and changing," he said. "It's like building a house on quicksand—the foundation isn't stable." But the writer commented sadly, "Try telling that to a young girl who believes the route to happiness is looking perfect, just like her favorite stars."[3]

Reading about sixteen-year-olds getting breast implants so they can look like their favorite star shocks me. But it shouldn't. Because I'm not all that different. If I had to choose between having Elisabeth Elliot's purity or J. Lo's body, I'd definitely pause—and grieve—before making the right choice. Great bodies and bulging bank accounts can be very alluring. Who wouldn't want to look like a cover girl, spend vacations in paradise, and be romanced by every man you meet—at least for a day or two?

Nothing New Here

> *What has been is what will be, and what has been done is what will be done, and there is nothing new under the sun.* Ecclesiastes 1:9

I doubt Moses did any dirty dancing, wore conspicuous gold jewelry, or had surgical augmentation to improve his appearance, but he still must have seemed larger than life to the early Christians. Stories about his brave adventures had probably grown more dramatic with each passing decade. I can just picture it: His *Desert Chronicles* were popular bedtime reading, and an enterprising Hebrew network was developing a reality show based on his life, pitting men and women against the elements in an arid region near the Egyptian border. Little boys hung posters of Moses—wearing a fierce expression and holding stone tablets high over his head—on their bedroom wall, and little girls dreamed of growing up and marrying someone just like him.

During the difficult times of the first century—when courage and perseverance were critical commodities—Jewish Christians probably thought about Moses more than ever. They remembered stories of how he had defeated Pharoah's finest and led their ancestors through the Red Sea to freedom. They recounted his steadfast determination throughout those forty years in the desert. And while they were reminiscing, it seems that they turned their attention away from Jesus. They started contemplating how nice it would be to revert back to the relative safety of Judaism, to the heritage of men like Abraham, King David, and Moses.

The Hebrews' gentle pastor is sympathetic with their nostalgia. He understands their longing for the good old days of enjoying harvest festivals with friends and attending the Vacation Torah School plays put on by their children. He doesn't malign the past or slander Judaism. Nor does he vilify their heroes; he simply compares Moses' humanity to the divinity of Jesus.

He affirms the legitimacy of Moses' leadership, both politically and spiritually. Moses was like a

Jewish George Washington, Abraham Lincoln, and Billy Graham rolled into one. He wore the mantle of Jehovah's blessing well. But the author of Hebrews reminds his flock that Moses was still human, and his greatness pales next to the perfect, incarnate Son of God.

> *So, my dear Christian friends, companions in following this call to the heights, take a good hard look at Jesus. He's the centerpiece of everything we believe, faithful in everything God gave him to do. Moses was also faithful, but Jesus gets far more honor. A builder is more valuable than a building any day. Every house has a builder, but the Builder behind them all is God. Moses did a good job in God's house, but it was all servant work, getting things ready for what was to come. Christ as Son is in charge of the house. Now, if we can only keep a firm grip on this bold confidence, we're the house!* Hebrews 3:1-6 (*The Message*)

Moses was faithful in God's house—Jesus built the house.

Moses was a servant in God's house—Jesus reigns supreme over it.

Moses testified to what God would do—Jesus is the revelation of the testimony.

Permanently Perfect

My friend's eleven-year-old son, Greg, is a football fanatic. He plays in a youth league, watches ESPN religiously, keeps track of several teams' statistics, and attends every high school, college, and pro game he can. So you can imagine how excited Greg was when Nashville got its very own NFL team, the Tennessee Titans. He covered his walls with their pictures and begged for jerseys for his birthday and Christmas. His dad purchased tickets for most of the home games, and I got used to the sight of Greg in blue face paint. I thought he'd be a Smurf look-alike for good when the Titans made it to the Super Bowl! But the next year the team had a so-so season and their halo started slipping.

As the losses continued to mount, Greg's football heroes began to lose their place in his mind. The posters came down, playing cards were traded, and the blue jerseys were shoved to the back of the closet. His exuberant faith in his favorite team really eroded during that difficult season. I had to bite my lip to keep from grinning when he soberly confided that he "just wasn't into the Titans" anymore.

Much like Greg, the Hebrews seemed to be turning into fair-weather fans. The difficulties they were facing had begun to dim their adoration for Jesus. They were tired of defeat and sick of being harassed; they wanted to win again. They became wistful about easier, more successful seasons with different coaches. They started peeling the poster of the great Lion of Judah off their walls and began rinsing off the paint of devotion. And that's when their mentor stepped in to stop their slide toward faithlessness.

Ever been there? Have you ever wished for a different kind of "coach," one who didn't demand a

lifetime of selflessness and blind faith and lugging crosses?

I have. Every now and then when I can't see around the corner of my circumstances or when I feel alone or misunderstood, I whine for a different kind of Messiah. One who will make all my messes disappear. One who will answer my prayer for a husband and children. One who will make my closest friends interested listeners, conscientious encouragers, and fatter than me. Sometimes I just wish our Hero of a Savior would make my life less hard.

Of course, a Savior like that only exists in fairy tales and isn't really very heroic. A Messiah who only serves to grant our wishes would be akin to an overly indulgent mother who lets her child eat all the candy he wants, stay up as late as he likes, and never makes him accept responsibility or obey authority. Pretty soon she's got a middle-aged man with no job, no friends, and no respect for her still living in his boyhood room and demanding Twinkies for lunch. And if we had a Messiah like that, we'd be no better off.

Blaise Pascal, a famous French theologian and mathematician in the 1600s, said, "God created man in His own image and then we returned the favor." In what specific ways do you think you've caricaturized God?

Jesus didn't die to make us happy. He's not some cartoon character flitting around in a sparkly outfit and waving a magic wand. He's not Cinderella's godmother. He's the sovereign Son of the Most High God. And He sacrificed His life because that was the only way to reconcile sinners like us with that very same God. Jesus died so we could get to know our heavenly Father. The dreams He fulfilled for us are much grander than the confines of our finite imaginations.

Hebrews reminds us of the things we should look for in a champion. Because whether we look up to Martin Luther, Martin Luther King Jr., Martin Scorsese, or Moses, they all have clay feet. They all make mistakes and tumble off pedestals. We have to keep our eyes on Jesus. He's the only one who deserves the distinction of *hero*.

Who has been a "Moses" in your life—someone who epitomized faithful spiritual leadership? How has his or her life impacted yours? (Extra credit: Write that person a letter thanking him or her for modeling the gospel for you.)

Then I turned to see the voice that was speaking to me, and on turning I saw seven golden lampstands, and in the midst of the lampstands one like a son of man, clothed with a long robe and with a golden sash around his chest. The hairs of his head were white like wool, as white as snow. His eyes were like a flame of fire, his feet were like burnished bronze, refined in a furnace, and his voice was like the roar of many waters. In his right hand he held seven stars, from his mouth came a sharp two-edged sword, and his face was like the sun shining in full strength.

When I saw him, I fell at his feet as though

dead. But he laid his right hand on me, saying,
"Fear not, I am the first and the last, and the
living one. I died, and behold I am alive forever-
more, and I have the keys of Death and Hades."

Revelation 1:12-18

Contrast John's vision of Jesus in Revelation
1:12-18 with the tender Messiah who gathered
children close to Himself (Matthew 19:13-15).
Are you more comfortable with the "Lion" or
the "Lamb" side of Jesus? Why?

5

Busyness Isn't a Spiritual Gift

Read Hebrews 4

The next section of the Hebrews sermon reminds
me of my favorite Starbuck's "after coffee" mints.
They're really little but very strong, kind of like
Altoids on steroids. On several occasions I've given
them to a friend, who pops one in her mouth only
to spit it out a few seconds later with an accusing
glance at me as if I had handed her an arsenic
lozenge! But I really do like the sweet and spicy
combination. Plus they give you good breath for
about two weeks!

The end of Hebrews 3 and most of Hebrews 4
might cause a contrasting sensation as well,
because the message is both comforting and
convicting. It's comforting because it explains
God's generous gift of rest. And it's convicting
because so few of us open His gift! It's also a multi-

faceted discourse because several types of rest are discussed.

First, there's the *creation rest* God took on the seventh day:

> *For he has somewhere spoken of the seventh day in this way: "And God rested on the seventh day from all his works."*   Hebrews 4:4

Then we read about the *Canaan rest* Joshua led the Israelites into after Moses was buried on Mount Nebo:

> *For if Joshua had given them rest, God would not have spoken of another day later on.*
>
>   Hebrews 4:8

There's also the *weekly* or *Sabbath rest* God gives His people:

> *So then, there remains a Sabbath rest for the people of God, for whoever has entered God's rest has also rested from his works as God did from his.*
>
>   Hebrews 4:9-10

And finally we see the *eternal rest* of salvation God promises to all those who believe in Him:

> *Since therefore it remains for some to enter it, and those who formerly received the good news failed to enter because of disobedience, again he appoints a certain day, "Today," saying through David so long afterward, in the words already quoted, "Today, if you hear his voice, do not harden your hearts."*   Hebrews 4:6-7

Busting through Busyness

Since few of us are foolish enough to claim we've created anything other than a mess, and since Canaan was the geographical inheritance for God's theocratic state, Israel, we're going to focus most of our attention in this chapter on the final two species of rest: Sabbath and eternal. But before we go any further, I need to give a disclaimer, because for me to write about rest is like Donald Trump waxing poetic about the joys of poverty. Resting isn't one of my strong suits—I'm what you might call rest-impaired. And my default setting has been on "Go" for as long as I can remember.

When I was in junior high and high school, I spent most weekends at my father's ranch, which was in central Florida in the middle of nowhere. The ranch was a great place to ride horses and motorcycles, chase roosters and fireflies. The only downside to life on the ranch was its isolation and the lack of friends my age.

Fortunately, several slightly wild kids from the youth group at Persia Baptist Church befriended me. It was one of the most interesting groups I had encountered. Gene had jet-black, John-Travolta-in-*Saturday-Night-Fever* hair, and he had the swagger to pull it off. Jimmy was the local lothario with a penchant for fast cars and cute girls. Chris was a country boy with a strong arm and dreams of playing college football. Karen was cool because her parents had European accents and cooked food we couldn't pronounce. And LuAnn was my more-experienced mentor in the art of dating and makeup. Needless to say, this delightful group of delinquents was more than glad to tutor a straitlaced city girl in the art of mild rebellion.

One of the more memorable incidents from my life of crime involved a pickup truck full of green oranges, a passing VW Bug, and peer pressure. It was a hot summer afternoon and we had all piled into the back of Chris's truck to go get Cokes from Roach's Grocery. (I'm not making this stuff up— that really was the name of the convenience store, and the tiny community where it was located was called Roachville.) The store was about five miles from my dad's ranch, and we chatted and threw oranges at street signs while Chris drove. We weren't planning to do anything destructive . . . until a little red bubble appeared on the horizon of County Road 46A, getting bigger and rounder as we barreled toward it. It looked like a rolling bull's-eye. Someone leaned down and scooped up a shirt full of oranges to hurl at the Bug, and we all followed suit. Everyone's fruity ammo missed the mark and bounced harmlessly off the blacktop, until the very last orange was tossed—the one I threw! Mine hit the road in front of the oncoming car and bounced up for a direct hit in the middle of the windshield.

The other driver slammed on his brakes and whipped around in hot pursuit as we jumped up and down in the back of the truck screaming as if our lives depended on outrunning him. But an old truck full of teenagers is no match for a Beetle bent on revenge; he caught up with us quickly. Still we yelled for Chris to keep driving. "Come on, Chris, keep going! Faster, faster!" Although we had

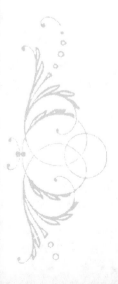

probably topped out at thirty miles per hour and the Volkswagen was inches from the rear bumper, we didn't want to stop because the forward motion kept us from facing reality. But after a mile or so we finally pulled over, and I hung my head to confess to the irate driver. Then we turned the truck around and wobbled back home—without so much as a Slurpee—to face my dad.

While I don't make a habit of hurling citrus in traffic anymore, I still tend to race as fast as I can through each day. And my frenetic activity fits right in to most Christian circles. We tend to wrap verses around our inability to rest, and we call it a virtue. We emphasize the "go out and do" passages but ignore the "be still and know" parts. We wear signs of physical exertion like badges of honor, as if all our stress "on God's behalf" is adding up like frequent-flier miles. And the busiest beavers in church are often labeled the best— until their exhaustion begets disillusionment and they limp away seeking a less demanding pond. There is no shortage of believers desperate for relief and restoration after being ridden too hard by the church. Frankly, some of the most stressed-out, emotionally spent people I've ever met are employed in full-time Christian ministry.

Take Time to Pause

Hebrews reminds us that busyness isn't a spiritual fruit, and perpetual motion is definitely *not* a virtue. God's people aren't supposed to resemble manic hamsters on spinning wheels; we're supposed to resemble Him.

*So then, there remains a Sabbath rest for the people
of God, for whoever has entered God's rest has also
rested from his works as God did from his.*

Hebrews 4:9-10

These words from the New Testament point to the
very beginning of the Old Testament, a book
Jewish Christians were more than familiar with.

*And God saw everything that he had made, and
behold, it was very good. And there was evening
and there was morning, the sixth day. Thus the
heavens and the earth were finished, and all the
host of them. And on the seventh day God finished
his work that he had done, and he rested on the
seventh day from all his work that he had done. So
God blessed the seventh day and made it holy,
because on it God rested from all his work that he
had done in creation.*   Genesis 1:31–2:3

Isn't it comforting to know that God crashed out
on a celestial couch after creating the universe? So
why in the world do we arrogantly assume rest is a
sign of spiritual slouching when God Himself
models it? He also mandates it:

*The LORD said to Moses, "You are to speak to the
people of Israel and say, 'Above all you shall keep
my Sabbaths, for this is a sign between me and you
throughout your generations, that you may know
that I, the LORD, sanctify you. You shall keep the
Sabbath, because it is holy for you. Everyone who
profanes it shall be put to death. Whoever does any
work on it, that soul shall be cut off from among*

*his people. Six days shall work be done, but the
seventh day is a Sabbath of solemn rest, holy to the
LORD. Whoever does any work on the Sabbath day
shall be put to death. Therefore the people of Israel
shall keep the Sabbath, observing the Sabbath
throughout their generations, as a covenant
forever. It is a sign forever between me and the
people of Israel that in six days the LORD made
heaven and earth, and on the seventh day he rested
and was refreshed.'" And he gave to Moses, when
he had finished speaking with him on Mount
Sinai, the two tablets of the testimony, tablets of
stone, written with the finger of God.*

Exodus 31:12-18

Wow, the Sabbath was serious business! This
passage makes it clear that it wasn't just tradition or
ceremony that caused the Israelites to rest on the
seventh day—these rules were *"written with the
finger of God."* Can you imagine what it would be
like if we still observed Old Testament law in
modern evangelical society? Most of us would be six
feet under! I'm so thankful Jesus redeemed us from
the Law and we don't have to fear being zapped for
mowing the lawn on Sunday. However, I also think
we've thrown the baby out with the bathwater by
ignoring the reason God stipulated a rest day in the
first place. And we've paid the price in peace.

God's Word reveals that He rested, commanded
His children to rest, declared that the land needed
rest, made provisions for unwitting criminals to
rest, and even planned a yearlong party to celebrate rest.

Rest wasn't negotiable for the Israelites, nor should it be for Christians. It's as clear a command from God as the Big Ten. The Sabbath isn't some punitive decree from a megalomaniac trying to take all the fun out of gardening on Sunday; it's God's merciful allowance for our protection.

His purpose for rest is not unlike wise car maintenance: We get the oil changed, water added, tires rotated, and the engine tuned so that our cars *don't* overheat or have a mechanical breakdown. But if you're trying to add water while steam billows around you and an angry line of cars backs up behind you, it's probably too late. In much the same way, if the only rest you're getting is more like collapsing, it's a sure bet that something's going to go seriously wrong with your spiritual engine.

More Info

To read more about God's plan for rest, see Leviticus 25:1-5 and 10-12, as well as Joshua 20:1-3.

If you had to assign a temperature to your life right now, based on the pressure and the pace, what do you think it would be? Are you close to overheating?

Disobedience and Rest Don't Mix

When I was growing up, my mom didn't allow me to watch scary movies, but my stepmother, Lucy, didn't have the same parenting parameters. I'll never forget the first horror movie she took my stepbrother, Ricky, and me to. It was called *The Boy Who Cried Werewolf.* For months after watching it, I wouldn't go into the barn because I was

convinced there was a hairy man-eater hiding in
the hayloft. I started riding my horse bareback and
putting her bridle on in the pasture so I wouldn't
be ambushed in the tack room!

My mother couldn't understand why I was
having such a hard time sleeping when I came
home from being with my dad and stepmother at
the ranch, especially since I had never been a fearful child and had always gone to bed without any
problem. She didn't know I had disobeyed her
no-scary-movies rule and couldn't get the vision of
carnivorous monsters out of my head!

Ever notice how the guilt of unconfessed sin is
more effective than caffeine in keeping you awake
at night? The lesson I learned as a ten-year-old has
echoed throughout my life: *rebellion and rest are
mutually exclusive.*

> *Who were those who heard and yet rebelled? Was
> it not all those who left Egypt led by Moses? And
> with whom was he provoked for forty years? Was
> it not with those who sinned, whose bodies fell in
> the wilderness? And to whom did he swear that
> they would not enter his rest, but to those who were
> disobedient? So we see that they were unable to
> enter because of unbelief.* Hebrews 3:16-19

Have you done something recently you knew
God didn't approve of and tossed and turned as
a result? Contrast the physical and emotional
differences between *rebellion* and *rest*.

The Israelites didn't have mutinous matinee
issues, but they were defiant stinkers in the wilder-

ness. When Moses took too long conferring with God on Mount Sinai, the people decided to throw a whopper of a party, and at the same time they threw faithfulness out the window. They made a cow out of metal and began to worship their sculpture instead of Jehovah. And though God had miraculously fed them with honey-flavored manna, they still begged to return to slavery because they missed those Egyptian all-beef patties with special sauce. They spent the better part of their Freedom Tour whining, complaining, and driving Moses crazy. But when Canaan eventually appeared on the horizon, they learned there were severe consequences for their rebellion. They were excluded from the Promised Land and never tasted the infinite liberty they had been so hungry for. Their sinful behavior sealed them to a fate of aimless wandering in the desert instead of resting in God's provision and protection.

Read Hebrews 3:7-19; Psalm 95:7-11; and Numbers 13 and 14. What is one of the specific rebellions the Israelites committed in the desert that the author of Hebrews is referring to in 3:16?

When I lived in Colorado I spent some time with a friend of a friend—I'll call her "Becky" for the sake of confidentiality—who was vehemently critical of Christianity. When Becky found out I worked for Focus on the Family, I might as well have told her that I clubbed baby seals for a living. The proverbial gloves came off and she prepared

for battle! She was very intelligent and articulate and liked to try and goad me into debates about abortion, "conservative" politics, or anything else she thought might spark an argument. I tried not to tangle with her, because she would eventually calm down and we'd always have really interesting conversations. Sometimes she dropped her guard enough to ask earnest questions about Jesus. Even the most hardened atheists usually soften when we listen to the Holy Spirit and treat them with the respect everyone created in God's likeness deserves.

Anyway, while Becky was diametrically opposed to Christianity, she wasn't exactly sure what she *did* believe in. She dabbled in Eastern mysticism, in meditation and crystals and Scientology, but none of her ingénue religious pursuits lasted for very long. She roamed restlessly from one thing to another because, despite the campaign promises of other belief systems, none can provide true eternal rest. Other faiths provide hoops for converts to leap through in a quest toward higher devotion and supposed enlightenment. But the aspiration for purification, absolution, salvation, and ultimate peace apart from Jesus is futile.

> *Jesus said, "I am the Road, also the Truth, also the Life. No one gets to the Father apart from me."*
> John 14:6 (*The Message*)

Read Ephesians 1:3. What do you think are the main differences between eternal rest in the "heavenly places" and the rest the Israelites had in Canaan after conquering the Promised Land?

Passionate Peace

Thankfully the Hebrews preacher doesn't ruminate on the consequences of unbelief for long before he gets back to the good news.

> *Let us therefore strive to enter that rest, so that no one may fall by the same sort of disobedience.*
>
> Hebrews 4:11

Read Hebrews 4:11-13 and 1 Corinthians 10:1-13. What's the central theme of these two passages? Describe the relationship between (better yet, find a metaphor for) accountability, obedience, and rest.

His words include an interesting juxtaposition: "strive to enter that rest." *Striving* and *rest* would appear to be mutually exclusive. *Webster's* defines *strive* as "to exert oneself vigorously; try hard."[1] Its definition of *rest* is "the refreshing quiet or repose of sleep; refreshing ease or inactivity after exertion or labor; relief or freedom, especially from anything that wearies, troubles or disturbs."[2]

Therefore, especially in light of the Old Testament Sabbath laws, we usually think of rest as a total time-out. Visions of sitting under a shade tree with a glass of lemonade and listening to soft harp music playing softly in the background come to mind.

God's Word does teach that periodic physical stillness is important for our well-being, but rest doesn't always manifest itself in couch-potato posture. This seeming contradiction in terms— *striving to enter rest*—broadens and clarifies God's

instructions. Restfulness isn't necessarily inactivity. As the author of Hebrews says, for Christians rest is the passionate, wholehearted pursuit of God. We can rest either sitting quietly in a field of flowers or running down a soccer field with a group of kids right on our heels!

Describe the most restful season of life you've ever experienced. What variables were present in that season which are missing from your life now?

Dr. John MacArthur elucidates this point when he says that *striving* (or being *diligent*, per his New King James Version Study Bible) emphasizes the accountability that comes to those who hear the Word of God.[3] The apostle James also accentuates the responsibility Christians have for active obedience:

> But be doers of the word, and not hearers only, deceiving yourselves. For if anyone is a hearer of the word and not a doer, he is like a man who looks intently at his natural face in a mirror. For he looks at himself and goes away and at once forgets what he was like. But the one who looks into the perfect law, the law of liberty, and perseveres, being no hearer who forgets but a doer who acts, he will be blessed in his doing.
>
> James 1:22-25

The word *retire* isn't in the Bible, but the word *rest* is sprinkled liberally throughout it. Sometimes its meaning involves a complete cessation of activity, as in the Old Testament Sabbath, and sometimes it doesn't. The Hebrews probably wished it did in their pastor's sermon. They probably thought they needed an extended vacation, that they deserved a hiatus from the prejudice and difficulty swirling around them. But their pastor doesn't advise them to go relax in a hammock by the beach this time; he tells them to stand firm in the face of persecution and to find rest by pressing toward God.

The same principle applies to us today. Just like those exhausted first-century believers, we will find contentment, peace, and confidence in our salvation in every situation in which we are moving toward God.

> *Are you tired? Worn out? Burned out on religion? Come to me. Get away with me and you'll recover your life. I'll show you how to take a real rest. Walk with me and work with me—watch how I do it. Learn the unforced rhythms of grace. I won't lay anything heavy or ill-fitting on you. Keep company with me and you'll learn to live freely and lightly.*
>
> Matthew 11:28-30 (*The Message*)

Share specific examples of how you've been encouraged or comforted by other believers recently. And share at least one relationship where God might want you to *give* encouragement and comfort.

6

The Certainty
of God's Calling

Read Hebrews 5–6

The first time I went skiing in the Rocky Mountains, I went with one of my closest friends, Judy, who had once been a ski instructor, and some of her ski instructor friends. Judy told them I was athletic, so they recommended that I skip the beginner slopes and head straight to the top of the mountain. I almost flattened a small child getting off the ski lift, but that didn't seem to faze them. I followed my friends past an ominous sign that read "Danger, Expert Terrain." Then they skied into a narrow, icy chute, obviously expecting me to follow. So I swallowed hard, pointed my skis down, and somehow flailed along behind them. But then we got to a precipice, and one by one, Judy's friends jumped gleefully over the edge. I stood there with my ski tips crossed and my mouth open, watching them carve perfect S-turns all the way down the slope until they were little dots at the bottom. I couldn't believe it—they were whooping in delight while I was fighting back the urge to scream for help.

Judy took one look at my face and knew I was in over my head. "Don't worry. I'll help you down; just follow me," she told me. Then she executed a video-worthy jump-turn off the cornice and swooshed down to a spot about fifty feet below me. All I could think was, *Here I am courting death when I should be flirting with cute ski instructors on the bunny slope!* But Judy was a compassionate teacher. While her friends skied off into the sunset, she spent two hours coaxing me down the mountain. She even had to carry me a few times so I wouldn't tumble down the side of the cliff we were traversing!

Read Hebrews 5:11-14. If our *sanctification* (growing in holiness, becoming more Christ-like) is solely dependent upon God's grace, then what do you think the author means by "the mature, who . . . have trained themselves to distinguish good from evil" (v. 14, NIV)? What part can we play in our own spiritual growth process? Describe the difference between training yourself to distinguish good from evil and works-based righteousness.

It seems the Hebrews needed a lot of coaxing, too.

> *About this we have much to say, and it is hard to explain, since you have become dull of hearing. For*

*though by this time you ought to be teachers, you
need someone to teach you again the basic principles
of the oracles of God. You need milk, not solid food,
for everyone who lives on milk is unskilled in the
word of righteousness, since he is a child. But solid
food is for the mature, for those who have their
powers of discernment trained by constant practice to
distinguish good from evil.*

*Therefore let us leave the elementary doctrine of
Christ and go on to maturity, not laying again a
foundation of repentance from dead works and of
faith toward God, and of instruction about
washings, the laying on of hands, the resurrection
of the dead, and eternal judgment. And this we
will do if God permits.*

Hebrews 5:11–6:3

**Read Hebrews 6:1-3. The phrase "go on to
maturity" is a weak translation from the literal
Greek, which actually reads "Let us *be carried
on* to maturity." Share an experience when God
"carried" you through a particularly rough
season and taught you deep biblical truths in
the process. (Remember the famous "Footprints" poem? This is your unique "Footprints"
story!)**

Their beloved teacher sends his students to deten-
tion with a stern reprimand about their spiritual
immaturity. Then he urges them to grow up, and
his exhortation—"Let us . . . go on to maturity"—is
significant. It's in the passive tense in the original
Greek language (*pheromai*) and literally means "Let

us *be carried on* to maturity."[1] As Christians, we can't journey toward spiritual maturity alone any more than I could ski in expert terrain as a beginner. Regardless of how many retreats we've attended, how many Bible studies we've completed, or how many underlines we have in our Bibles, we can't make it by ourselves. We are utterly dependant on God to increase our wisdom, faith, and righteousness. Paul says it well in his letter to those unruly Corinthians:

> *For consider your calling, brothers: not many of you were wise according to worldly standards, not many were powerful, not many were of noble birth. But God chose what is foolish in the world to shame the wise; God chose what is weak in the world to shame the strong; God chose what is low and despised in the world, even things that are not, to bring to nothing things that are, so that no human being might boast in the presence of God. He is the source of your life in Christ Jesus, whom God made our wisdom and our righteousness and sanctification and redemption. Therefore, as it is written, "Let the one who boasts, boast in the Lord."*   1 Corinthians 1:26-31

Just like us, Jewish Christians in the first century were sometimes spiritual pygmies. They were slow to learn basic biblical truths and fearful about their future. And they had good reason to be afraid—ending up as citronella torches at one of Nero's garden parties was a distinct possibility because of their status as heretics. So while their spiritual instructor chastises them for childish behavior, he also tenderly reminds them they aren't alone, that God will carry them into a deeper walk with Him.

Bare Arms and Bad Theology

Read Hebrews 6:4-6. What's your initial emotional response to this passage? Why?

After emphasizing our total reliance on Christ, the Hebrew pastor throws his parishioners—and us—a curveball.

> *For it is impossible to restore again to repentance those who have once been enlightened, who have tasted the heavenly gift, and have shared in the Holy Spirit, and have tasted the goodness of the word of God and the powers of the age to come, if they then fall away, since they are crucifying once again the Son of God to their own harm and holding him up to contempt. For land that has drunk the rain that often falls on it, and produces a crop useful to those for whose sake it is cultivated, receives a blessing from God. But if it bears thorns and thistles, it is worthless and near to being cursed, and its end is to be burned.*
>
> Hebrews 6:4-8

Reread 6:4-6 and list at least four attributes regarding the type of people the author is referring to (e.g., they've been *enlightened*).

This passage raise a chilling question: Does this mean you can lose your salvation?

My friend Helen grew up in the forties and fifties. She attended a very conservative church full of mostly kind, well-intentioned people. But when she came home from college in a short-sleeved dress, her salvation was questioned. Some—including her pastor—thought Helen had lost her salvation because she'd been brazen enough to show her elbows in worship. My mother attended a similar church after she got married, and her salvation was questioned because she wore earrings and lipstick. I wonder how the people who misjudged Helen and my mom would handle the tank tops and belly rings some modern Christian women wear!

Of course, not everyone who believes you can fall from grace is an old-fashioned grouch, overly concerned with uncovered appendages and Estée Lauder. Some very smart, sincere Christians and well-respected Bible scholars (most of whom know considerably more about God's Word than I do) firmly believe you can lose your salvation. Denominations have been formed and churches have split over this issue. Needless to say, we won't be able to cover all the theological positions and complexities of this passage. But we will wrestle with the question it begs: *Is it possible for Christians to lose their salvation?*

First we need to note the danger of balancing an entire doctrine on the slender shoulders of just one passage. We need to consider the entirety of Scripture when it comes to questions as significant as the security of our salvation. And there are many other passages in God's Word that point to the permanence of our relationship with Christ.

My sheep hear my voice, and I know them, and they follow me. I give them eternal life, and they will never perish, and no one will snatch them out of my hand. My Father, who has given them to me, is greater than all, and no one is able to snatch them out of the Father's hand. John 10:27-29

Who shall separate us from the love of Christ? Shall tribulation, or distress, or persecution, or famine, or nakedness, or danger, or sword? As it is written, "For your sake we are being killed all the day long; we are regarded as sheep to be slaughtered." No, in all these things we are more than conquerors through him who loved us. For I am sure that neither death nor life, nor angels nor rulers, nor things present nor things to come, nor powers, nor height nor depth, nor anything else in all creation, will be able to separate us from the love of God in Christ Jesus our Lord. Romans 8:35-39

In him you also, when you heard the word of truth, the gospel of your salvation, and believed in him, were sealed with the promised Holy Spirit, who is the guarantee of our inheritance until we acquire possession of it, to the praise of his glory. Ephesians 1:13-14

Read Romans 8:31-39 and John 10:25-30. Compare these passages with Hebrews 6:4-6. Do you think they are "contradictory" or "complimentary" passages?

These biblical examples certainly seem to shout a loud *no* to the question of Christians losing their salvation, especially when we dig a little deeper. For instance, the phrase "they will never perish" in John 10 is very forceful in the original Greek and might be translated more explicitly, "they shall certainly not perish forever."[2] The Greek word for "guarantee" in the Ephesians passage on page 77 is a legal term that represents a payment obligating the contracting party (in this case, God) to make further payments.[3] This means we're in an ongoing relationship with God and brings to mind Paul's encouragement to the Philippians:

> *I am sure of this, that he who began a good work*
> *in you will bring it to completion at the day of*
> *Jesus Christ.*　　　　　　　　　　Philippians 1:6

I firmly believe that it will be a cold day in you-know-where before it's possible for a true believer in Jesus Christ to lose his or her salvation!

Close Only Counts in Horseshoes and Hand Grenades

So just what does our Jewish preacher mean when he talks about thorns and thistles and the impossibility of being restored again (Hebrews 6:4–8)? I think he's talking about people who *look* like Christians, and perhaps even *act* like believers for a season, but who never really put their faith in Christ alone for their salvation. And there's a perfect example of a couple like that in the book of Acts.

A man named Ananias, with his wife Sapphira,
sold a piece of property, and with his wife's knowl-
edge he kept back for himself some of the proceeds
and brought only a part of it and laid it at the apos-
tles' feet. But Peter said, "Ananias, why has Satan
filled your heart to lie to the Holy Spirit and to keep
back for yourself part of the proceeds of the land?
While it remained unsold, did it not remain your
own? And after it was sold, was it not at your
disposal? Why is it that you have contrived this deed
in your heart? You have not lied to men but to
God." When Ananias heard these words, he fell
down and breathed his last. And great fear came
upon all who heard of it. The young men rose and
wrapped him up and carried him out and buried
him.

After an interval of about three hours his wife
came in, not knowing what had happened. And
Peter said to her, "Tell me whether you sold the
land for so much." And she said, "Yes, for so
much." But Peter said to her, "How is it that you
have agreed together to test the Spirit of the Lord?
Behold, the feet of those who have buried your
husband are at the door, and they will carry you
out." Immediately she fell down at his feet and
breathed her last. When the young men came in
they found her dead, and they carried her out and
buried her beside her husband. And great fear
came upon the whole church and upon all who
heard of these things.   Acts 5:1-11

That story gives a whole new meaning to the
saying "Liar, liar, pants on fire"! Ananias and

Sapphira sure looked like Christians. They were bringing tithes and ceremoniously placing them at the disciples' feet. But contrary to their appearance, they weren't really righteous at all. They were actually conniving deceivers who hung out with New Testament believers but didn't have a saving relationship with Jesus Christ. Personality and proximity to other Christians doesn't equal salvation. Plenty have warmed a pew, walked an aisle, checked a card, or attended a Billy Graham crusade without really knowing God.

Remember Judas? He perfected the Christian facade down to the smallest detail and fooled everybody except Jesus for three years. Moral people can easily masquerade as Christians. But *looking* like a Christian doesn't mean you're counted among the redeemed.

Have you ever known someone who "looked" like a Christian for a period of time but then walked away from the faith? Do you think he or she was really a Christian to begin with? Explain why or why not. Who's another biblical example (besides Ananias, Sapphira, and Judas) of someone who looked like a believer but then renounced his/her faith?

Charles Spurgeon wrote a sermon on Hebrews 6:4-6 aptly titled "A Letter to the Almost Converted." He believed that these verses point to those among the Jewish believers who weren't actually Christians. They may have entertained the idea of Jesus as the promised Messiah, but when the going got really tough, they caved in. They

renounced Christ because they weren't willing to die for something they weren't fully committed to.

Many Bible scholars refer to this passage as a *real hypothesis*. They believe that the pastor is using superlative semantics to alert his congregation to the danger of apostasy—falling away from faith in Christ—even though apostasy is impossible for true Christians. It's kind of like the way I warn my best friend's little boys about becoming "pancakes" when they think they're too big to hold my hand while crossing the street. They won't actually morph into breakfast food; I'm just trying to motivate them to watch out for careless drivers piloting three-ton SUVs. I believe the exaggerated semantics in chapter 6 are meant to motivate the Hebrews—and us—to be spiritually alert.

Well-known writer F. F. Bruce says, "If the Bible teaches perseverance of the saints, it also teaches that it is the saints who will persevere." However, my all-time favorite quote regarding this passage in Hebrews doesn't come from a famous author, but from a wise pastor, Arch Warren, who shepherds a church near Nashville. He says, "Those who fizzle at the finish were faulty at the first." Not multisyllabic, theological terminology, but just as profound!

Hanging On to Hope

The author of Hebrews goes on to graciously affirm a nonfizzling finish for his dear ones.

> *Though we speak in this way, yet in your case, beloved, we feel sure of better things—things that belong to salvation. For God is not so unjust as to*

overlook your work and the love that you showed
for his sake in serving the saints, as you still do.

Hebrews 6:9-10

**In light of the strong language in Hebrews
6:4-6, what do you think the author was emphasizing in 6:9-12?**

Then he concludes the lesson by telling them
they can take God's promises to the bank:

> *So when God desired to show more convincingly to*
> *the heirs of the promise the unchangeable character*
> *of his purpose, he guaranteed it with an oath, so*
> *that by two unchangeable things, in which it is*
> *impossible for God to lie, we who have fled for*
> *refuge might have strong encouragement to hold*
> *fast to the hope set before us. We have this as a sure*
> *and steadfast anchor of the soul, a hope that enters*
> *into the inner place behind the curtain, where Jesus*
> *has gone as a forerunner on our behalf, having*
> *become a high priest forever after the order of*
> *Melchizedek.*

Hebrews 6:17-20

**The Greek word (*nothros*) translated "sluggish"
in 6:12 also means "slow to learn." In what spiritual "subject" would you say you've been a
slow learner?**

While I was working for Focus on the Family, I
was part of a national women's conference series
called Renewing the Heart. Our conferences were

similar to Promise Keepers events, but instead of thousands of men in a football stadium, ours featured thousands of women in indoor arenas. One year (Renewing the Heart enjoyed fourteen conferences over a three-year period) I thought it would be a good idea to rappel into the arena after lunch. You see, women tend to get a little sleepy by the afternoon session and need something to wake them up. Plus I thought it would be a fun way to demonstrate the fact that you don't have to be boring to be a Christian! My boss, Dr. Dobson, wasn't too keen about the stunt because he didn't savor the idea of me becoming a pancake, but after I assured him that I was taking safety precautions, he reluctantly agreed.

Jerry, an experienced union "flyer" who swings through the rafters of arenas all over the world in order to attach sound system cables and speakers, was assigned to help me. We decided our debut would take place at the inaugural conference of the year in Greenville, North Carolina. I wasn't nervous at first because I had rappelled in the mountains a few times and I thought this would be similar. But when I followed Jerry up a flimsy metal ladder onto a swaying, chicken-wire walkway, my confidence evaporated. He told me to follow him to the very edge of the walkway and then casually told me to hop up on the railing so he could fasten me into the harness. We were more than a hundred feet in the air above a cement floor. I really wished he had already fastened me into something—something like a big elevator going down!

But when the band started to play the song

signaling the beginning of this never-before-attempted-at-a-Christian-women's-conference stunt, I knew that backing out would ruin the whole program. So I grabbed the rail with sweaty hands and gingerly slid over the side. When Jerry saw that I was literally trembling with fear, he held my hand and said gently, "You don't have to be afraid; everything's going to be okay." Then he clipped me into my harness and told me the rope I was holding on to was tested to ten thousand pounds and was attached to the steel girders that held up the roof of the coliseum. He said all I had to do was hang on to the rope because the steel wouldn't budge. I had blisters afterward to prove just how tightly I held on!

Even steel beams are toothpicks compared to the strength and stability of our heavenly Father.

> *We who have run for our very lives to God have every reason to grab the promised hope with both hands and never let go. It's an unbreakable spiritual lifeline, reaching past all appearances right to the very presence of God where Jesus, running on ahead of us, has taken up his permanent post as high priest for us, in the order of Melchizedek.*
>
> Hebrews 6:18-20 (*The Message*)

Nothing can break the relationship we have with God in Christ. Nothing can collapse His love for us. Don't get so distracted by the difficult verses in the middle of this chapter that you miss the promise at the end: *God will never fail us.*

7

A Man Named Mel

Read Hebrews 7–8

When I was in junior high, I had four heroines: Jill, Kelly, Sabrina, and Jaime. Charlie's Angels and the Bionic Woman. The angels had better hair and more believable plotlines, but Jaime Sommers was still my favorite. She had bionic legs and could run as fast as a car; she also had a bionic ear and could hear the conversations of criminals a mile away! And when she wasn't making pensive faces or flirting with Lee Majors, she was single-handedly making the world a better place. At first glance Jaime looked like a normal person—well, like a normal *actress*—but she wasn't. She was created in a top-secret government lab and had superhuman capabilities.

The next section of Hebrews describes a high priest who, like Jaime Sommers, was not at all like other human priests.

*For this Melchizedek, king of Salem, priest of the
Most High God, met Abraham returning from the
slaughter of the kings and blessed him, and to him
Abraham apportioned a tenth part of everything.
He is first, by translation of his name, king of righteousness, and then he is also king of Salem, that is,
king of peace. He is without father or mother or
genealogy, having neither beginning of days nor
end of life, but resembling the Son of God he
continues a priest forever.*

*See how great this man was to whom Abraham
the patriarch gave a tenth of the spoils! And those
descendants of Levi who receive the priestly office
have a commandment in the law to take tithes from
the people, that is, from their brothers, though these
also are descended from Abraham. But this man
who does not have his descent from them received
tithes from Abraham and blessed him who had the
promises. It is beyond dispute that the inferior is
blessed by the superior. In the one case tithes are
received by mortal men, but in the other case, by one
of whom it is testified that he lives. One might even
say that Levi himself, who receives tithes, paid
tithes through Abraham, for he was still in the
loins of his ancestor when Melchizedek met him.*

Hebrews 7:1-10

**Read Genesis 14:17-24. Based on this passage,
what do Melchizedek and Jesus have in
common?**

Hmmm . . . that's about as easy to understand as
the directions to program my PDA! Much has been

made about this character Melchizedek, who takes up a lot of ink in Hebrews. And his notoriety in the New Testament is fascinating when you consider how few words are used to describe him in the Old Testament:

> *After his return from the defeat of Chedorlaomer and the kings who were with him, the king of Sodom went out to meet him at the Valley of Shaveh (that is, the King's Valley). And Melchi-zedek king of Salem brought out bread and wine. (He was priest of God Most High.) And he blessed him and said, "Blessed be Abram by God Most High, Possessor of heaven and earth; and blessed be God Most High, who has delivered your enemies into your hand!" And Abram gave him a tenth of everything.*
>
> Genesis 14:17-20

> *The LORD has sworn and will not change his mind, "You are a priest forever after the order of Melchizedek."* Psalm 110:4

Why do you think Abraham paid a tithe to Melchizedek, even though the commandment to tithe hadn't been given to Moses yet? What emotions or circumstances help you to *want* to tithe?

That's it. All the narrative about Melchizedek is summed up in those four tidy verses in Genesis and one sentence from David. Yet the extended depiction of him in Hebrews has stumped the best and brightest Bible students among us. Many people think this "mystical Mel" stuff is just too weird to decipher, but it's not nearly as strange as it seems.

Why do you think David writes about the priesthood of Melchizedek when the Levitical (Aaronic) priesthood had been established and in place for at least 350 years? What makes Melchizedek different from the Levite priests?

I don't think the pastor is trying to be coy or confusing here. He probably uses Melchizedek as an illustration *because* of the brevity of his story in the Old Testament. Since his encounter with Abraham doesn't mention his genealogy or lifespan, he's the perfect allegorical example to make the point that Jesus wasn't like the human high priests the Jews were familiar with.

did you know?

Much like the Bionic Woman, Melchizedek seems to have superhuman qualities. For example:

His title—king of Salem—means "king of peace." Jesus is called the "Prince of Peace" (Isaiah 9:6).

Mel is from nowhere, metaphorically—"without father or mother or genealogy" (Hebrews 7:3). Jesus was born of a virgin.

Mel's reign seemed to be timeless. Scripture tells us that Jesus will reign forever (Revelation 11:15).

Mel's death wasn't recorded. Jesus was resurrected to live forevermore at the right hand of the throne of God.

Finally, even though he was a priest, Mel wasn't invited to the Levitical family reunions. Jesus was not from the tribe of Levi either (Matthew 1:1-17).

A Continuation of Clay Feet

I recently attended a women's conference that bore an eerie resemblance to my last trip to Las Vegas. In Sin City I had seen a steady stream of tourists sit at slot machines for hours on end. Most looked eager at first, hoping the next quarter would trigger a jackpot. Their eyes reflected bright neon lights while scanning spinning lines of fruit. But after a while, their enthusiasm was replaced by escalating disappointment as their stack of coins shrank with each pull on the handle.

At the women's conference, in an auditorium full of potted plants and good intentions, I watched a steady stream of Christian women line up to be touched by a well-known speaker. She claimed to be a prophet anointed by God, and perhaps she was, but the words she spoke sure didn't sound like they came from Him. Her voice rose dramatically as she forecast pregnancies for menopausal women, material riches for those in financial ruin, and fame for others. Some of her "prophecies" seemed so irresponsible in light of the desperate woman standing in front of her, I felt sick to my stomach. I wondered if she ever called the women she'd prayed for to see how they were doing when the fortunes she told didn't come true. Did she ever weep with the infertile women whose wombs remained empty in spite of her words? Did she ever write a check to the women who believed God would give them millions but still weren't sure how to feed their families?

It broke my heart to watch those women flock to

FAST FACT

By the way, Mel's name is pronounced mel-KIZZ-e-deck, and it's a fun word to nonchalantly toss out at church suppers just to see what kind of reaction you get!

a flashy performer and ostensibly walk right past God's promises in the process. The temptation to follow enigmatic leaders rather than Jesus is the basis for the following lesson about His superiority to the Aaronic priesthood:

> *Now if perfection had been attainable through the Levitical priesthood (for under it the people received the law), what further need would there have been for another priest to arise after the order of Melchizedek, rather than one named after the order of Aaron? For when there is a change in the priesthood, there is necessarily a change in the law as well. For the one of whom these things are spoken belonged to another tribe, from which no one has ever served at the altar. For it is evident that our Lord was descended from Judah, and in connection with that tribe Moses said nothing about priests.*
>
> *This becomes even more evident when another priest arises in the likeness of Melchizedek, who has become a priest, not on the basis of a legal require-ment concerning bodily descent, but by the power of an indestructible life. For it is witnessed of him, "You are a priest forever, after the order of Melchizedek."*

Hebrews 7:11-17

The gist of this lecture is that people aren't perfect like Jesus, not even the priests who lead us. Whether your spiritual mentor is more tangibly gifted than anybody else you've met, heard, or seen on televi-sion, that person is still a sinner. Even if your pastor/priest/preacher/teacher/prophet can predict

events in the future, write best-selling books, move
you to tears, or do backflips off the pulpit, that
person still can't save you. Jesus shed the same
amount of blood at Calvary to redeem those people
as He did for poor wretches like you and me.

We need to quit bowing at the altar of mortal
charisma.

**Read Hebrews 7:18-25. What specific character-
istics make this hope "better" than the former
regulation?**

Stretch Limos and a Superior Savior

Last summer I joined several friends on a trip to
New York. It was our friend Cindy's fiftieth birthday, and her husband's gift to her was a no-expense-
spared trip to the Big Apple with her buddies. A
stretch limousine picked us up at the airport and
whisked us to lavish suites in a five-star hotel across
from Central Park. So as to defeat even the slightest
symptoms of jet lag, we had aromatherapy massages
and facials right away. The first morning of our
dalliance with decadence started with a scrumptious
breakfast in a world-famous restaurant frequented
by movie stars, followed by ultraexpensive haircuts
and manicures at a trendy salon. We were so tired
from all the pampering that we had to take a nap
before being escorted to our gourmet dinner and
center seats at an award-winning Broadway musical
that evening!

Our utopian trip with Cindy was unlike any trip
I've ever taken, and I made a few mental notes as
a result. I decided that being carted around in a

private limousine with a chivalrous, anecdotal driver is much better than being jostled about in a taxi driven by a non-English-speaking madman. A facial administered gently by a classically trained aesthetician, with scents customized to my mood, is much better than scrubbing with an old washcloth at home. And scrambled eggs with fresh herbs and a cappuccino at the Plaza are definitely better than coffee and an Egg McMuffin at Mickey D's.

Needless to say, my return to Nashville brought with it a crushing kind of culture shock. No one swooped in wearing a jaunty black cap to carry my luggage. My house hadn't been miraculously beautified, enlarged, or cleaned by elves while I was away. And my hair settled into an eighties-style helmet in response to the humidity. I sorely missed all the "better than" luxuries I'd grown so fond of.

The Hebrews were also tired and disillusioned. Following Jesus was proving to be harder than they had thought. Some were even tempted to return to the soothing familiarity of priests and Jewish rituals. So their concerned pastor concludes chapter 7 with a long list of "better than" facts about Jesus:

> *The former priests were many in number, because they were prevented by death from continuing in office, but he holds his priesthood permanently, because he continues forever. Consequently, he is able to save to the uttermost those who draw near to God through him, since he always lives to make intercession for them.*

For it was indeed fitting that we should have
such a high priest, holy, innocent, unstained,
separated from sinners, and exalted above the
heavens. He has no need, like those high priests, to
offer sacrifices daily, first for his own sins and
then for those of the people, since he did this once
for all when he offered up himself. For the law
appoints men in their weakness as high priests,
but the word of the oath, which came later than
the law, appoints a Son who has been made
perfect forever.   Hebrews 7:23-28

The first item in our Savior's "more than a cut
above catalog" is His *immortal permanence.* One of
my college professors retired the week after our
final exam, and we all wished it had been a semes-
ter sooner. The class was much more difficult than
it needed to be because of her infirmity. Her mind
had deteriorated with age, and she just couldn't
communicate clearly anymore, especially when it
came to quantitative statistics! But our Messiah's
mind will never decay, His eyesight won't dim, His
memory won't fade. He will never change! James
speaks to that immutability in his epistle:

Every good gift and every perfect gift is from
above, coming down from the Father of lights
with whom there is no variation or shadow
due to change.   James 1:17

Read Hebrews 8:3-6. What's significant about
the Tabernacle (called the Tent of Meeting
prior to the building of Solomon's Temple)
being called "a copy and shadow" of heaven?

Jesus' changelessness makes Him superior to human priests because He will never grow old and die!

Secondly, unlike human priests, Jesus is *morally flawless.* I attended a large church in college led by a very successful pastor. He wrote books that flew off the shelves and was captivating on the radio and television. Our fellowship grew by leaps and bounds as a result of his dynamic leadership. But people were devastated when it was discovered that he'd been having a long-term affair with a woman in the congregation. His betrayal crippled the church.

Propitiation
an atoning sacrifice that gains the favor and goodwill of God

Skim Exodus 25–27. God's instructions are incredibly detailed. Why didn't He just give them architectural and decorating carte blanche when it came to building the Temple?

But we never have to wonder if Jesus is cavorting with the choir director. We don't have to modify our confession to Him because we're afraid our sins will be broadcast over the golf course. We don't have to be ashamed because our Messiah leaves such miserly tips at Shoney's after church on Wednesday night. We'll never walk into the sanctuary to find our Savior sobbing at the altar because of His transgressions. Jesus doesn't have to make sacrifices for Himself. He is holy, innocent, and unstained. Jesus is superior to human priests because He is sinless!

The third item is Jesus' *definitive treatment of sin.* We don't have to walk down the aisle every Sunday to be saved all over again. When Jesus offered Himself up on the cross, sin was taken

care of once and for all. In Hebrews, Christ's death is called a "propitiation," which means His sacrifice turned away the wrath of God, thereby making God favorable toward us:

> *Therefore he had to be made like his brothers in every respect, so that he might become a merciful and faithful high priest in the service of God, to make propitiation for the sins of the people.*
>
> Hebrews 2:17

And the propitiation this verse refers to is conclusive. John's Gospel records Jesus saying, "It is finished," just before bowing His holy head in death (John 19:30). Furthermore, the single Greek word translated into those three words Christ uttered before dying on the cross had been found on ancient tax receipts, meaning "paid in full."[1] Our sinful debts were wiped out with the precious blood of God's only Son. Our bondage is over, the fat lady has sung, and Elvis has left the building!

Jesus is superior to human priests because His death was the final, perfect sacrifice.

The fourth and final item in this inventory of Jesus' more excellent attributes is His *infinite sovereignty*. We don't have to cross our fingers and hope this good luck will last. Our heavenly Father has appointed His Son to a reign without any term limits!

My sister's oldest son, Jordan, was eager to

More Info

Check out these two other verses in the New Testament that use the word *propitiation*:

He is the propitiation for our sins, and not for ours only but also for the sins of the whole world. (1 John 2:2)

In this the love of God was made manifest among us, that God sent his only Son into the world, so that we might live through him. In this is love, not that we have loved God but that he loved us and sent his Son to be the propitiation for our sins. (1 John 4:9-10)

start school this year but was anxious about who his teacher would be. Would it be a man or a woman? Would the teacher be young or old? strict or lenient? I can sympathize with Jordan's anxiety because I remember walking into class one year on the first day of school and realizing that the unsmiling tyrant with thick glasses and thicker ankles was going to ruin the next nine months of my life! But we don't have to worry who our "new savior" is going to be, whether he'll pronounce our name correctly, be nice to us or generous with hall passes, because Jesus won't quit, retire, or be fired from His position as our Messiah. His reign will never end!

> *Then the seventh angel blew his trumpet, and there were loud voices in heaven, saying, "The kingdom of the world has become the kingdom of our Lord and of his Christ, and he shall reign forever and ever."*
>
> Revelation 11:15

 If you could have your way (think outside the parameters of "proper theology" for a minute!), what would heaven be like?

Jesus is superior to human high priests because He will reign forever.

And forever with Jesus promises to be a wonderful time.

Read 2 Corinthians 5:17 and Hebrews 8:13. The word *obsolete* in Hebrews 8 comes from the Greek word *palaioō*, which also means "to wear

out or become old." What habits or activities from your "BC life" (before you became a Christian) now seem old and worn out? Share something in particular that used to bring you momentary happiness or satisfaction but no longer has any appeal now that your hope is in Christ.

8

Red Is the Color of Redemption

Read Hebrews 9

You can't throw a rock without hitting a musician
in Nashville. Every restaurant is filled with food
servers who dream of hitting it big in the music
industry. I've seen wait staff at restaurants in other
cities cringe in embarrassment when they have to
sing "Happy Birthday" to a diner, per the bistro
tradition. But waiters here practically knock each
other down trying to get to the celebrating table in
order to belt out their best rendition of "Happy
Birthday." They're hoping to catch the eye and ear
of any producer who might be dining nearby!
However, I've discovered that being a professional
singer isn't as glamorous as it appears. It requires a
lot of hard, monotonous work. Of course, I didn't
find this out from personal experience—I'm a
misfit in Music City and can't carry a tune in a
bucket—but from friends who literally sing for
their supper.

My closest friend, Kim, has released fourteen contemporary Christian albums and I have every single one! She is currently working on a new Christmas project, and I stopped by the recording studio last week to bring her some lunch. They were just finishing up a song when I walked in. Jamie, the producer, signaled to me that it would just be a minute, so I sat down quietly to listen. But lunch got cold, because Kim had to sing the exact same line over and over again for the next hour. Every time she sang it, Jamie said something like, "Yeah, that sounds great." And for a moment I was sure she was about to be set free from the isolation booth. But then he would press the intercom and tell her to try it one more time, with some tiny variation of a note or intonation. I'm sure Kim will be able to sing that song pitch-perfect for the rest of her life because the melody must have been permanently engraved in her brain by the time she left the studio. Frankly, by the time I had listened to her sing the same thing fifty times in a row, I think I could have recorded it!

The pastor of Hebrews is somewhat like Jamie the record producer because he seems to be telling his flock the same thing over and over again. He begins his sermon by explaining Jesus' superiority to the old revelation from God. He segues into an explanation about Jesus' superiority to angels, then he reveals Jesus' superiority to the Law and their Jewish folk hero, Moses. This is followed by a justification of the superior position Jesus commands over human priests. And now here we

are, past the halfway point of his message, and it's still the same declaration: Jesus is *better*!

Coke Isn't the Only Real Thing

Chapters 8 and 9 of Hebrews celebrate how Christ's ministry really is better than anything we've known previously.

> *Now the point in what we are saying is this: we have such a high priest, one who is seated at the right hand of the throne of the Majesty in heaven, a minister in the holy places, in the true tent that the Lord set up, not man. For every high priest is appointed to offer gifts and sacrifices; thus it is necessary for this priest also to have something to offer. Now if he were on earth, he would not be a priest at all, since there are priests who offer gifts according to the law. They serve a copy and shadow of the heavenly things. For when Moses was about to erect the tent, he was instructed by God, saying, "See that you make everything according to the pattern that was shown you on the mountain." But as it is, Christ has obtained a ministry that is as much more excellent than the old as the covenant he mediates is better, since it is enacted on better promises. For if that first covenant had been faultless, there would have been no occasion to look for a second.* Hebrews 8:1-7

The last time I went to New York—a much less extravagant trip than my previous lifestyles-of-the-rich-and-famous vacation—my friend Libby wanted to visit Canal Street. For those of you who've never been there, Canal Street is a dingy thoroughfare that houses a flurry of activity, most of it involving the sale of counterfeit goods. Side-by-side storefronts advertise a plethora of fake items, including "Rolex" watches and "Louis Vuitton" luggage. At first Libby seemed taken aback by the cacophony of bootleg rap music, cab horns, and screaming vendors hawking their products. But she was intent on finding the perfect purses for loved ones back home, so she squared her shoulders and plunged bravely into the sea of commercial debauchery.

We traipsed through store after store until we found what looked to be the best place to purchase forgeries. (Did I mention that we were in town for a Christian women's retreat?) Libby started sifting through the inventory with the skeptical eye of a veteran—she learns fast—when the proprietor of the store approached us aggressively. She asked if we wanted to see her "best" merchandise, the stuff reserved for "special" customers. I've always been partial to being called special, plus I was a little intimidated, so I said yes while Libby just looked on in silence. Then the woman said, "You wait here, no move, no call police," and disappeared. I was instantly nervous—I wasn't even the one shopping, and here I was being lured into some kind of nefarious, illegal handbag operation! Before I could think clearly enough to make a run for it, the bossy lady reappeared carrying a black garbage bag. She grabbed me by the arm and said, "You come here, no do in open," and whisked me through a small closet door behind the "Nike" display. Hoping for Narnia, I instead found myself trapped in a tiny

bathroom with a snarling saleswoman I couldn't understand.

I did make it out of that little lavatory physically unscathed, but I was flustered enough to learn my lesson: I won't ever cruise imitation alley again. Besides, the "Kate Spade" purse I bought was a big waste of money. Even though it looked like the real thing, the leather was actually pleather, the lining wasn't sewn correctly, and the whole thing fell apart the first time it got wet!

Although the Tent of Meeting that the Old Testament Israelites carted around and the beautiful Temple Solomon built in Jerusalem were based on divine blueprints, they were still just copies—sincere forgeries, if you will—of the heavenly tabernacle that is God's dwelling place. The desert gazebo and stone structure were simply patterns of the real thing. Even the sacred sacrificial system was a prototype. It was supposed to provide atonement for sin, connection to God, and a clear conscience. But at best it really only offered limited access to those things.

Read Hebrews 9:1-14 and skim Exodus 40. More than forty chapters in the Old Testament talk about the Tabernacle. Why do you think this is so important to understand? Which verse in the Hebrews passage best indicates this for you?

These preparations having thus been made, the priests go regularly into the first section, performing their ritual duties, but into the second only the high priest goes, and he but once a year, and not

*without taking blood, which he offers for himself
and for the unintentional sins of the people. By this
the Holy Spirit indicates that the way into the holy
places is not yet opened as long as the first section is
still standing (which is symbolic for the present
age). According to this arrangement, gifts and
sacrifices are offered that cannot perfect the
conscience of the worshiper, but deal only with food
and drink and various washings, regulations for
the body imposed until the time of reformation.*

Hebrews 9:6-10

These verses became vivid reality during my last trip to Israel a few years ago. We were in Jerusalem on Yom Kippur—the Day of Atonement—which is what the above passage describes when it says, "But into the second only the high priest goes, and he but once a year, and not without taking blood, which he offers for himself and for the unintentional sins of the people." That day is the highest holy day in the Jewish calendar. A solemn occasion, even moderately committed Jews observe Yom Kippur.

When our guide dropped us off at the hotel so he could get home before sunset on Yom Kippur, I asked him what the appropriate greeting was for the evening. He explained that the greeting was in the form of a question—*Gamar Hatima Tova*—meaning, "Will you be inscribed with a good inscription?" Then he said, "Lisa, we don't believe in grace and mercy the way you do. We believe in God's justice. And we hope that by remembering all the ways we've transgressed His law over the

past year, we'll receive justice instead of wrath."
His answer is one of the saddest commentaries on
the weakness of religious ritual I've ever heard. It
was a living illustration of the old system's inability to perfect the conscience of the worshipper.

If only that wonderful man could wrap his mind
and heart around the much better—perfect—sacrifice we have in Christ.

---

did you know?

Here's a short list of Yiddish phrases:

Gamar Hatima Tova (pronounced: ga-MAR ha-TEE-mah TOE-vah):
"Will you be inscribed with a good inscription?" This question is posed
like a greeting before Yom Kippur.

Shalom Shabbat (pronounced: sha-LOME sha-BAHT): "Peaceful
Sabbath." This is a blessing given before the Jewish Sabbath (you'll hear
it a lot on Friday afternoon in a Jewish neighborhood).

A Gezunt Dir in Pupik (pronounced: ah Geh-SOONT dear
enPOOHP-ik): "Good health to your belly button." This is a blessing and
is intended to wish health to your whole system—not just your belly
button!

A Broch (pronounced: ah-BROOKH): Basically a Jewish bad word or
curse. It's a way of saying you're at your wit's end!

Bobbeh Meisseh (pronounced: BOH-bah MY-she): "Grandmother's
Tale." This has the same general meaning as an "old wives' tale."

Oy Veh (pronounced: oy-VAY): An expression of exasperation like,
"Oh no!"

Mecheieh (pronounced: meh-KHY-eh): "It's a pleasure!" This is what
you'd exclaim if you found a twenty-dollar bill that you didn't know was
in your pocket.

Kishkes (pronounced: KISH-kess): "Guts" or "Intestines." This word is
figuratively used to describe emotion that comes from the deepest part of
your body. If I ever get engaged, I'm going to feel happiness from the
kishkes!

When Christ appeared as a high priest of the good things that have come, then through the greater and more perfect tent (not made with hands, that is, not of this creation) he entered once for all into the holy places, not by means of the blood of goats and calves but by means of his own blood, thus securing an eternal redemption. For if the sprinkling of defiled persons with the blood of goats and bulls and with the ashes of a heifer sanctifies for the purification of the flesh, how much more will the blood of Christ, who through the eternal Spirit offered himself without blemish to God, purify our conscience from dead works to serve the living God. Hebrews 9:11-14

Compare Hebrews 9:7 with Hebrews 9:14. Try to describe what it might feel like to only be forgiven once a year. How does this challenge you regarding what we have in verse 14?

There Really Is Power in His Blood

One of my favorite Old Testament stories provides the backdrop for Hebrews 9. It also helps us to understand the importance of the blood of Christ and many of the old hymns we sing but don't necessarily understand.

After these things the word of the LORD came to Abram in a vision: "Fear not, Abram, I am your shield; your reward shall be very great." But Abram said, "O Lord GOD, what will you give me, for I continue childless, and the heir of my house is Eliezer of Damascus?" And Abram said, "Behold, you have given me no offspring, and a member of my household will be my heir." And behold, the word of the LORD came to him: "This man shall not be your heir; your very own son shall be your heir." And he brought him outside and said, "Look toward heaven, and number the stars, if you are able to number them." Then he said to him, "So shall your offspring be." And he believed the LORD, and he counted it to him as righteousness.

Genesis 15:1-6

Abraham (God changes his name in Genesis 17) is depressed because he and his wife, Sarah, don't have any children and they're both so old they're wearing Depends. Then God says, "Cheer up and drive on over to Target for Pampers because you're going to have a houseful of children!" That's not literal Hebrew, but it's pretty close! And Abraham believed God . . . at first. But remember, Abraham was just a man. He wasn't perfect; he was a sinner just like the rest of us. He wasn't a righteous man before God called him to faithfulness. Don't forget the tale he'd recently told Pharaoh about Sarah: "Yeah, my 'sister' is pretty hot—you can have her!" (Genesis 12:10-20). He risked his wife's reputation—perhaps even her life—in order to save his own skin. So it should come as no surprise that Abraham's trust in God's grandiose promises ebbs away quickly.

And he said to him, "I am the LORD who brought you out from Ur of the Chaldeans to give you this land to possess." But he said, "O Lord GOD, how am I to know that I shall possess it?"

Genesis 15:7-8

Do you ever feel like Abraham did? "Okay God, I've read all these amazing promises in the Bible, but I don't see any of them coming true in my life. How can I be sure that You will really provide for me and protect me and never leave me?"

God's patience with our questions is amazing, and what He did next to prove His faithfulness to Abraham is the reason Jesus' blood is so precious:

> *He said to him, "Bring me a heifer three years old, a female goat three years old, a ram three years old, a turtledove, and a young pigeon." And he brought him all these, cut them in half, and laid each half over against the other. But he did not cut the birds in half. And when birds of prey came down on the carcasses, Abram drove them away. . . .*
>
> *When the sun had gone down and it was dark, behold, a smoking fire pot and a flaming torch passed between these pieces. On that day the LORD made a covenant with Abram, saying, "To your offspring I give this land, from the river of Egypt to the great river, the river Euphrates, the land of the Kenites, the Kenizzites, the Kadmonites, the Hittites, the Perizzites, the Rephaim, the Amorites, the Canaanites, the Girgashites and the Jebusites."*
>
> Genesis 15:9-11, 17-21

This animal dissection ceremony that seems so strange to us wasn't odd to old Abraham. It was a familiar ancient custom that served as a "covenant" or agreement between two parties.[1] Remember, it wasn't a literary culture; there were no written words, much less attorneys or jokes about attor-

neys! So they used colorful—sometimes shocking—symbolism to communicate what we now use
computers and legal jargon to accomplish. And this
messy ritual was just as binding as a "No Escape
Clause" contract. By cutting the animals in half, the
two parties were symbolizing what should happen
to them if they betrayed the blood covenant.

In his Old Testament journal, the prophet prone
to tears—Jeremiah—even refers to the gruesome
ramifications of breaking a blood covenant:

> *The men who transgressed my covenant and did*
> *not keep the terms of the covenant that they made*
> *before me, I will make them like the calf that they*
> *cut in two and passed between its parts.*

Jeremiah 34:18

The miracle of Abraham's story is that only one
of the two parties entering into the covenant
walked between the animal carcasses. Abraham is
sleeping like a baby when the smoking firepot and
flaming torch pass through the crimson furrow.
And in case you haven't guessed yet, the pot and
the torch are *theophanies.*

By walking through alone, God tangibly demon-
strated His own pledge: "If the covenant between
us is broken, I'll pay the price in My blood." Of
course, God knew we'd break our promises to Him.
That our faithfulness would wane. That we'd fuss
and fight with each other and resist His authority.

When God walked that lonely path to the tune
of Abe's snoring, He knew His Son would also walk
a path by Himself to pay the price for our rebellion.
God's agreement with Abraham is a foreshadowing

FAST FACT

A theophany is a
physical manifesta-
tion of God. What
other theophanies
can you think of
from the Old and
New Testaments?
(Hint: See Exodus
3 and 13:17-22.)

of Jesus' death on the cross. It points toward the red flow that poured from Christ's body—the blood that redeemed our sin so that the covenant between us and our heavenly Father could be restored.

There Is Power in the Blood

Would you be free from the burden of sin?
There's power in the blood, power in the blood;
Would you o'er evil a victory win?
There's wonderful power in the blood
There is power, power, wonder working power
In the blood of the Lamb;
There is power, power, wonder working power
In the precious blood of the Lamb.[2]

Compare Hebrews 9:20 with Exodus 24:6-8 and Matthew 26:26-28. (See also 1 Corinthians 11:23-28.) How do these verses alter or challenge your thoughts about the symbolism of Christ's blood during Communion? Would you make any personal change?

No More Marching

Every year at Yom Kippur, my friend who lives in Israel takes off his sandals and puts on tennis shoes because leather is traditionally eschewed on high holy days for being too comfortable. He walks—because riding in an automobile or even riding a bicycle would be considered "working"—to a big temple in downtown Jerusalem. And there he tries to remember every single time he's broken the law of God in the past year. He earnestly believes that this arduous task is what God demands from him.

There is no joy in this exercise, no perfecting of his conscience, and no sense of completion, because this will not be the last time he marches to temple to recount his sin. He knows he'll have to repeat the whole process all over again next year if he has any hope of receiving God's justice, let alone mercy.

Read Hebrews 9:15-28. Note how many times the words *blood* and *death* are used. How do these verses relate to the Crucifixion and the importance of His blood?

I couldn't do it. I can't remember all the times I sinned in the last week, much less in the last year. If my relationship with God depended on my memory or ritualistic repetition, I'd be in a lot of trouble. But it doesn't. There is a better road that leads to reconciliation with God. And Jesus died to pave it for us.

> ### More Info
>
> If you haven't seen *The Passion of the Christ*, rent it this weekend and consider exactly what it meant for Jesus to "put away sin by the sacrifice of himself" (Hebrews 9:26).

Thus it was necessary for the copies of the heavenly things to be purified with these rites, but the heavenly things themselves with better sacrifices than these. For Christ has entered, not into holy places made with hands, which are copies of the true things, but into heaven itself, now to appear in the presence of God on our behalf. Nor was it to offer himself repeatedly, as the high priest enters the holy places every year with blood not his own, for then he would have had to suffer repeatedly since the foundation of the world. But as it is, he has appeared once for all at the end of the ages to put away sin by the sacrifice of himself. And just as it is appointed for man to die once, and after that comes judgment, so Christ, having been offered once to bear the sins of many, will appear a second time, not to deal with sin but to save those who are eagerly waiting for him.

Hebrews 9:23-28

 In what ways would you describe the church you attend as a "copy" of what God has prepared for us in heaven? In what ways does your fellowship fall noticeably short of God's blueprint and feel more like a cheap imitation?

I'll bet those tired Hebrew believers were starting to see some light at the end of their tunnel. And I bet their toes were beginning to tap to the now-familiar tune of Jesus' superiority!

9

Torn Curtains and True Friends

Read Hebrews 10

The pastor of Hebrews divides chapter 10 like an experienced teacher. The first half is a review of the perfection and sufficiency of Christ's sacrifice, while the second half moves on to a new subject: the confidence available to us through Jesus. And though the first eighteen verses are wonderful, we're going to hurdle the review and jump right into the new stuff!

Read Hebrews 10:19-25. Underline each of the "let us" exhortations in these verses. Which one is especially meaningful to you? Why?

> *Therefore, brothers, since we have confidence to enter the holy places by the blood of Jesus, by the new and living way that he opened for us through the curtain, that is, through his flesh, and since we*

have a great priest over the house of God, let us draw near with a true heart in full assurance of faith, with our hearts sprinkled clean from an evil conscience and our bodies washed with pure water.

Hebrews 10:19-22

Three years ago, just before Easter, I was invited to attend the He Chose the Nails tour with Max Lucado and several Christian recording artists in Memphis. I was also privileged to receive a backstage pass that allowed me to move freely throughout the building. Ten thousand people attended this event at the Pyramid, a huge coliseum overlooking the Mississippi River, and most of them wanted to spend some time with Max. They wanted him to sign something or pose for a picture or listen to a story about how his books had influenced their life. Of course, many couldn't even get near him; the lines were just too long. I certainly didn't deserve special treatment, but because of that laminated card hanging around my neck, I didn't have to stand in line. I got to sit right next to Max and talk to him. While most of the people that day had to use a telephoto lens, I was able to have a one-on-one conversation with Max Lucado.

When Jesus opened a new way to God through His death on the cross, He left backstage passes for His beloved. You and I now have intimate access to the Creator of the universe because we've been marked by the blood of Christ. We don't have to loiter around a huge arena, hoping to catch a glimpse of God getting on a bus by the backstage door. We get to waltz right into His inner sanctum.

Deism
the belief in God as a distant, supreme authority who rules the universe from afar and has little or no interaction with the daily life of human beings

Furthermore, our exclusive passes aren't stamped "Friend" or "Acquaintance," they're stamped "F-A-M-I-L-Y," in bright red letters! And our special status isn't based on our deservedness; we get to draw near to God because we're His children.

Our world has long been full of people who believe in God but view Him as some kind of distant supreme being who doesn't bother Himself with the minutiae of humanity. Hebrews 10:22 blows holes in that false doctrine. God is intimately interested in the lives of His children, so much so that He allows us unrestricted admission to His presence. Remember, this is a new concept for the Hebrews. They weren't accustomed to having unlimited contact or close proximity to God. In their day, most ancient rulers were unapproachable by anyone but their highest advisors.[1] Consider this passage from the story of Esther:

> **More Info**
>
> To find out more about Esther—and the first recorded *extreme makeover* experience— read her biography in the Old Testament. It's sandwiched between Nehemiah and Job.

> *Then Esther spoke to Hathach and commanded him to go to Mordecai and say, "All the king's servants and the people of the king's provinces know that if any man or woman goes to the king inside the inner court without being called, there is but one law—to be put to death, except the one to whom the king holds out the golden scepter so that he may live. But as for me, I have not been called to come in to the king these thirty days."* Esther 4:10-11

That passage reminds me of how intimidated the Scarecrow, Tin Man, Cowardly Lion, and Dorothy were when they first stood before the Wizard of

Oz. They were convinced that the loud, reverberating voice represented a giant, mean magician. But then Toto pulled down the curtain to reveal a white-haired man with a twinkle in his eye.

When Jesus tore down the supernatural curtain separating us from God's presence, he revealed an awesomely holy and unexpectedly gracious Ruler. And because Jesus took the punishment we deserved on the cross, we don't have to tremble in fearful anticipation when we approach the throne of God. We can leap *confidently* into His lap (Hebrews 10:19)!

I love watching Kim's boys greet her when she returns home from a trip. Graham and Benjamin aren't tentative or hesitant when they see her car pull into the driveway. They usually race toward her like they've been shot from a cannon. They smother her in hugs and sticky kisses and usually hang on to her all the way into the house.

We should display that same delightful boldness when we head toward our heavenly Father. We don't have to inch forward cowering, as if He might punish us. Nor do we have to approach Him in a formal way, "more appropriate" manner, as if He might not remember us. We're His children! He loves us more than we can even imagine. He went to extraordinary lengths to be with us, and in response we should smother Him with whole-hearted affection.

 **Reread Hebrews 10:19-22. When you approach the throne of God are you a "lap leaper"? Or do you tend to approach God's throne with your**

knees knocking, afraid He's going to whack you with a giant trouble stick? List a few things you need to work on to improve your confidence in this area.

My Dad's Bigger than Yours

Not only should we be confident in our right to enter God's company, the shepherd of Hebrews reminds us that we should also be the most hopeful kids on the planet. And hope is certainly a fitting topic for this section, in light of the depressing situation the Hebrew Christians found themselves in.

> *Let us hold fast the confession of our hope without wavering, for he who promised is faithful.*
>
> Hebrews 10:23

I once read a great illustration of security and hope written by Robert Winnie, who tells the story of how, as a six-year-old boy, he was harassed by the neighborhood grouch, Mr. Bernhauser.

> *He was our backyard neighbor. He was especially mean and unfriendly to kids, but he was also rude to adults. He had an Italian plum tree that hung over the back fence. If the plums were on our side of the fence, we could pick them, but God help us if we got over the fence line. . . . He would scream and yell at us until one of our parents came out to see what the fuss was about. Usually it was my mother, but this time it was my father. No one liked Mr. Bernhauser very much, but my father was particularly against him because he kept all the*

*toys and balls that had ever landed in his yard. So
there was Mr. Bernhauser yelling at us to get . . .
out of his tree, and my father asked him what the
problem was. Mr. Bernhauser took a deep breath
and launched into a diatribe about thieving kids,
breakers of rules, takers of fruit, and monsters in
general. I guess my father had had enough, for the
next thing he did was shout at Mr. Bernhauser
and tell him to drop dead. Mr. Bernhauser stopped
screaming, looked at my father, turned bright red,
then purple, grabbed his chest, turned gray, and
slowly folded to the ground. I thought my father
was God. That he could yell at a miserable old
man and make him die on command was beyond
my comprehension.*[2]

I'm sure Robert Winnie's confidence in his
father's "supreme" authority waned when he got
older, when he discovered that his dad couldn't
really make people expire at will, or always keep
him safe, or control the universe. But our divine
adoptive Dad *can* do all those things! He is the
sovereign King of kings and Lord of lords. And
He's promised to be faithful to His children. That's
why we can hang on to hope, no matter what.

The Order to Encourage

I've heard that it takes twenty positive comments
to counteract one negative remark. I'm not sure if
this statistic is based on scientific analysis or not,
but it sounds about right to me. I know it sure took
a lot of encouragement to offset some of the nasty
barbs I received.

When I was a sophomore in high school, I tried

out for the girls' varsity basketball team. They had a lofty past, so I was thrilled to make the cut and surprised to earn a starting position. I was nervous when it came time for our first home game and we jogged out of the locker room and found the stands crammed with enthusiastic fans. My mom waved an orange and black pom-pom, and my boyfriend beamed from the top row of the bleachers.

A few minutes into the game, someone passed me the ball. I stood there shell-shocked. A teammate tried to help by shouting, "Shoot it, Lisa! Shoot it!" So I shot it, but it didn't swish cleanly through the net like I had imagined it would. As a matter of fact, it missed the net and the backboard completely. My first chance at the sports hall of fame, and I launch an airball in front of five hundred people! Immediately a heckler started up—my very own Mr. Bernhauser. He screamed that I was terrible, that I didn't deserve to wear a Seminole uniform, and that I needed to be benched. He even yelled at the other players when they threw me the ball again. His insults were harsh, especially considering that he was a school administrator. And I didn't know it at the time, but besides being a basketball enthusiast, he was also an alcoholic, which explains his lack of tact.

When it came time for me to walk up to the line to take two free throw shots, his slurs echoed throughout the gym: "She'll never make it! She couldn't hit the broadside of a barn! Get her off the court!" I think most people were holding their breath along with me, just hoping I would make the basket so he would stop yelling and sit down.

I'm sure I prayed something like this before letting the first ball fly: *Lord, if You'll just help me make this, I'll go to Africa as a missionary!* It looked like the shot was going in at first, but then it rolled off the rim and fell to the floor. The heckler was even louder during my second attempt. "She won't make this one either! Send in a sub, coach!" And although I had made thousands of free throws in our backyard, I missed again. I was so humiliated; I wanted to cry and run off the court. I didn't, but I didn't play basketball after that season either. My adolescent ego was no match for an assistant principal's drunken taunts.

Read Proverbs 16:24-25 and 18:21. Look back over your behavior during the past few months and consider whether or not you've wounded someone by tossing out a discouraging or ugly remark. Pray about how to go about asking forgiveness and making amends.

My experience playing high school volleyball was exactly the opposite because of a woman named Donalyn Knight. Her title was Coach, but her calling was to encourage kids. We beat teams that were much more athletically gifted because we never gave up! No matter how intimidating our opponent was, we always believed we had a chance to win. And even when we lost, Coach Knight cheered until she was hoarse and treated us like heroes anyway. I graduated more than twenty years ago, but Donalyn Knight still calls and e-mails me on a regular basis just to make sure I'm doing okay and to see if I have any prayer requests.

Her affirmation continues to spur me on, especially
when I'm up against a circumstance that feels
bigger than me.

The following verse reminds me of her:

> *And let us consider how to stir up one another to
> love and good works, not neglecting to meet
> together, as is the habit of some, but encouraging
> one another, and all the more as you see the Day
> drawing near.*

Hebrews 10:24-25

**Reread Hebrews 10:24-25. Who
would you name as your own
personal Donalyn—someone who
encourages you regularly? Have you
ever written that person a card or a
letter expressing how much their
affirmation means to you? If not,
consider doing that this week.**

More Info

For an interesting look at a
biblical character who epitomized encouragement, read
about Barnabas, whose name
means "son of encouragement."
His story can be found in Acts
11–15.

If you were graded on how many encouraging
words you speak into the lives of others, would you
pass or fail?

The pastor in Hebrews makes it clear that our
mouth, mind, and heart should bend toward the
benefit of others. And he explains that we can't do
it in seclusion. We need to meet together in order
to be encouraged (v. 24).

**What kind of Christian community do you
have? Would you describe it as a small,
tight-knit band of brothers and sisters who are**

committed to love one another well—even when it hurts—so as to honor the Lord? Or does it feel more like a cruise ship, where everyone smiles and acts like they're having a good time, but they're actually emotional strangers?

A good friend was deeply wounded and offended by some fellow members in our church. As a result, she decided to find another place to worship. When she told me she was changing churches, she said, "I'm so sick of this! I just want to be in a church where I can worship God but not have to be around people." I could relate to her emotions; I've felt like forsaking the inevitable frustration in Christian relationships a few times myself. Sometimes the vision of worshipping in pajamas and passing a plate to myself is appealing. But avoiding all contact with the body of Christ isn't the best solution. We need one another, even though we get on each other's nerves and step on each other's toes! There's no such thing as a Lone Ranger in the royal priesthood. Jesus makes that clear in John's Gospel:

> *A new command I give you: Love one another.*
> *As I have loved you, so you must love one another.*
> *By this all men will know that you are my disciples,*
> *if you love one another.*   John 13:34-35 (NIV)

DVD **Read John 13:34-35 again. Who is the poster child for those verses in your life? Do you think other people would describe you as a "lover of people"?**

Of course, that doesn't mean we're going to be soul mates with every one we meet at church either. Frankly, the megachurches of our culture aren't very conducive to the kind of relationships the pastor of Hebrews is advocating. It's hard to connect on a heart level with someone when you have to look at his or her name tag first.

In his book *Waking the Dead,* John Eldredge exposes the farce of finding intimacy among the masses with this question: Would you feel comfortable turning to the person in the pew next to you and, as you pass the offering plate, asking him to bind a demon that is sitting on your head?[3]

He goes on to elaborate about the necessity— and pain—of authentic community:

> *Living in community is like camping together. For a month. In the desert. Without tents. All your stuff is scattered out there for everyone to see. C'mon—anybody can look captured for Christ an hour a week, from a distance, in his Sunday best. But your life is open to those you live in community with. Some philosopher described it like a pack of porcupines on a winter night. You come together because of the cold, and you are forced apart because of the spines.*[4]

Only a few friends know me intimately. They're familiar with my weaknesses, insecurity, and pride. Sometimes they point them out so as to push me closer to Christ. But sometimes they bruise me because of their own junk. It's not always easy being real because no human friendship is perfect or completely safe. Plus I'm not always comfortable confessing sin and asking for prayer. Superficial interaction with other churchgoers is less complicated. But I wouldn't trade those rare close friendships for all the dark chocolate in the world because I've been encouraged to love God more deeply as a result of their love for me.

Do you socialize with other church members out of habit or guilt? Or do you connect with a small "band of brothers" out of prayerful intentionality? Are you committed to stay in relationship even after someone's sharp quills poke you right in the heart?

Don't Toss Your Trust

The pastor encourages the Hebrews with warm memories about their perseverance in order to help them hang on in the present.

> *But recall the former days when, after you were enlightened, you endured a hard struggle with sufferings, sometimes being publicly exposed to reproach and affliction, and sometimes being partners with those so treated. For you had compassion on those in prison, and you joyfully accepted the plundering of your property, since you knew that you yourselves had a better possession and an abiding one. Therefore do not throw away your confidence, which has a great reward. For you have need of endurance, so that when you have done the will of God you may receive what is promised. For, "Yet a little while, and the coming one will come and will not delay; but my righteous one shall live by faith, and if he shrinks back, my soul has no*

*pleasure in him." But we are not of those who
shrink back and are destroyed, but of those who
have faith and preserve their souls.*

Hebrews 10:32-39

One of the most challenging things about high
school volleyball was the preseason workouts.
Freshman athletes had the hardest time adjusting
to the intensity of preseason workouts because they
didn't know what to expect. Sometimes one of
them would collapse in a pool of tears and perspira-
tion and say she just couldn't go any further. But
upperclassmen didn't give up because we knew
what would be required of us. We had passed
through volleyball purgatory before, so we were
confident we could survive it again. Experience
begets assurance.

The Hebrews were walking through something
they had endured with flying colors earlier. When
they had been persecuted for their faith in the
past, they had been faithful. They had stoically
tolerated public insults. They had visited fellow
Christians in prison, risking their own safety in the
process. They didn't complain when their property
was unfairly seized by spiteful countrymen. And
their coach reminds them here of those former
victories in order to kindle their confidence. He
wanted them to take a deep breath, pray for God's
help, and then stand firmly in the face of persecution once more.

10

Misfits, Martyrs,
and Miracles

Read Hebrews 11

The first half of Hebrews 11 is a lot like John 3:16. Most Christians—and even some unbelievers—are at least a little familiar with this section of Scripture commending the big kahunas of the faith: Noah, Abraham, Isaac, Jacob, Joseph, Moses, and red-ribbon Rahab. But the second half of this sermon-within-a-sermon on faith isn't nearly as recognizable. And neither are some of the "heroes" mentioned:

> *And what more shall I say? For time would fail me to tell of Gideon, Barak, Samson, Jephthah, of David and Samuel and the prophets—who through faith conquered kingdoms, enforced justice, obtained promises, stopped the mouths of lions, quenched the power of fire, escaped the edge of the*

sword, were made strong out of weakness, became mighty in war, put foreign armies to flight.

Hebrews 11:32-34

I can understand the inclusion of David, Samuel, and prophets like Daniel in this "Faith Hall of Fame," but I don't understand the induction of men like Gideon, Barak, Samson, and Jephthah. Their exploits aren't nearly as courageous as those of Noah and Moses. For instance, look at Gideon's initial response to God's calling:

Now the angel of the LORD came and sat under the terebinth at Ophrah, which belonged to Joash the Abiezrite, while his son Gideon was beating out wheat in the winepress to hide it from the Midianites. And the angel of the LORD appeared to him and said to him, "The LORD is with you, O mighty man of valor." And Gideon said to him, "Please sir, if the LORD is with us, why then has all this happened to us? And where are all his wonderful deeds that our fathers recounted to us, saying, 'Did not the Lord bring us up from Egypt?' But now the LORD has forsaken us and given us into the hand of Midian." And the LORD turned to him and said, "Go in this might of yours and save Israel from the hand of Midian; do not I send you?" And he said to him, "Please, Lord, how can I save Israel? Behold, my clan is the weakest in Manasseh, and I am the least in my father's house." Judges 6:11-15

Read Luke 6:27-36. To give grace (unmerited favor) to our *enemies* for the sake of the gospel can be as difficult as it is heroic. Can you think of a Bible character who exemplifies this? Are you close to any modern-day saints who are faithful about loving their enemies well? Explain.

This isn't a very auspicious beginning for someone referred to as a "mighty man of valor." Gideon acts more like a sissy than a soldier! When the angel discovers him, he's hiding in a wine barrel. Then he reveals immature theological understanding by questioning God's goodness in light of his struggles. And although God graciously overlooks his gaffes to say, "I'm choosing you to lead My people in battle," Gideon even tries to weasel out of that commission by claiming that he hasn't been working out lately and that he comes from a family of weaklings. In spite of Gideon's excuses, the Lord still uses him to accomplish His purposes. But this guy certainly doesn't personify faith!

The next unlikely champion listed in Hebrews is a guy named Barak, someone who also tried to wriggle out of military duty:

> *Now Deborah, a prophetess, the wife of Lappidoth, was judging Israel at that time. She used to sit under the palm of Deborah between Ramah and Bethel in the hill country of Ephraim, and the people of Israel came up to her for judgment. She sent and summoned Barak the son of Abinoam from Kedesh-naphtali and said to him, "Has not*

the LORD, the God of Israel, commanded you, 'Go, gather your men at Mount Tabor, taking 10,000 from the people of Naphtali and the people of Zebulun. And I will draw out Sisera, the general of Jabin's army, to meet you by the river Kishon with his chariots and his troops, and I will give him into your hand'?" Barak said to her, "If you will go with me, I will go, but if you will not go with me, I will not go."

Judges 4:4–8

Barak is a multi-starred-and-striped member of the armed forces. But he's also a big wimp. Instead of living up to the medals on his uniform, he balks when Deborah asks him to take the lead on upcoming maneuvers. He huffs a childish ultimatum: "You go first or I'm taking all my toys and going home!" And the ensuing Israelite victory is due more to Deborah's trust in Jehovah than Barak's bravery. Again, not exactly the behavior of someone who should be held up as an example of faithfulness.

Then there's my personal favorite: Samson. While he may not have received a dishonorable discharge from the literal military, his biggest mistakes occurred on the battlefield of romance.

After this he loved a woman in the Valley of Sorek, whose name was Delilah. And the lords of the Philistines came up to her and said to her, "Seduce him, and see where his great strength lies, and by what means we may overpower him, that we may bind him to humble him. And we will each give you 1,100 pieces of silver." So Delilah said to

Samson, "Please tell me where your great strength lies, and how you might be bound, that one could subdue you."   Judges 16:4-6

Before we get to the Paul Harvey part of Samson's sad story, we need to stop and look at the major mistake he made in the verses above. Delilah is a *Philistine* citizen; she was part of a people group who were archenemies of Israel. She lived in the Valley of Sorek, which can be translated as the "valley of grapes"[1] (*sorek* in Hebrew refers to vineyards). Samson was a Nazirite. That means he was supposed to be "set apart" for God's pleasure. According to his Nazirite vows, he was forbidden to enjoy the fruit of the vine: no raisins in his cereal or wine with dinner. Yet here he was, blithely courting a trashy girl from Grapeville. The enticing path of this forbidden courtship snaked right past a flashing warning sign from God. Yet Samson kept right on walking.

> **More Info**
>
> Want to know more about Samson and his Nazirite roots? Check out Judges 13.

And she said to him, "How can you say, 'I love you,' when your heart is not with me? You have mocked me these three times, and you have not told me where your great strength lies." And when she pressed him hard with her words day after day, and urged him, his soul was vexed to death. And he told her all his heart, and said to her, "A razor has never come upon my head, for I have been a Nazirite to God from my mother's womb. If my head is shaved, then my strength will leave me, and I shall become weak and be like any other man."

When Delilah saw that he had told her all his heart, she sent and called the lords of the Philistines, saying, "Come up again, for he has told me all his heart." Then the lords of the Philistines came up to her and brought the money in their hands. She made him sleep on her knees. And she called a man and had him shave off the seven locks of his head. Then she began to torment him, and his strength left him. And she said, "The Philistines are upon you, Samson!" And he awoke from his sleep and said, "I will go out as at other times and shake myself free." But he did not know that the LORD had left him. And the Philistines seized him and gouged out his eyes and brought him down to Gaza and bound him with bronze shackles. And he ground at the mill in the prison. Judges 16:15-21

Not only did Samson waltz right past the Lord's blinking caution light, he ignored Delilah's wicked schemes three times (Judges 16:6-14). She didn't even bother to apologize for his attempted murder; she just put on her best perfume and a low-cut dress and batted her eyelashes a fourth time. And this time he folds. I wonder what he was thinking when he finally realized that his girlfriend sold him out for silver.

The final member of this infamous group of faith heroes named in Hebrews is Jephthah.

Jephthah made a vow to the LORD and said, "If you will give the Ammonites into my hand, then whatever comes out from the doors of my house to meet me when I return in peace from the

Ammonites shall be the LORD's, *and I will offer it*
up for a burnt offering." So Jephthah crossed over
to the Ammonites to fight against them, and the
LORD *gave them into his hand. And he struck them*
from Aroer to the neighborhood of Minnith, twenty
cities, and as far as Abel-keramim, with a great
blow. So the Ammonites were subdued before the
people of Israel.

Then Jephthah came to his home at Mizpah.
And behold, his daughter came out to meet him
with tambourines and with dances. She was his
only child; beside her he had neither son nor
daughter. And as soon as he saw her, he tore his
clothes and said, "Alas, my daughter! You have
brought me very low, and you have become the
cause of great trouble to me. For I have opened my
mouth to the LORD, *and I cannot take back my*
vow."   Judges 11:30-35

I don't like this tragic story in Judges because
Jephthah's rash vow cost his only child her life. This
dumb daddy joins Gideon, the anxious barrel boy;
Barak, the yellow-bellied military officer; and
Samson, the clueless Romeo. These four men appear
much less deserving of respect, but a second look at
verse 34 reveals why they're included in the Faith
Hall of Fame: "who . . . were made strong out of
weakness."

It seems the pastor includes these less impres-
sive biographies mainly *because* of their flaws!
Don't forget that the ancient Hebrew believers
were struggling. They were wavering in the face
of political persecution and oppression. They were

scared, and some of them weren't just shrinking back—they were turning tail and running for their lives. They probably considered the testimonies of icons like Moses and thought, *Yeah, right. I could never trust God like he did. I would have drowned in the Red Sea!* But when their pastor recounts the "faith" of clearly flawed characters like Gideon and Barak, they realize that God can turn even wimps into valiant warriors. These examples reassured them that in spite of their fear, they too could stand firm in the face of persecution.

Aren't you glad God shares the stories of such flawed "heroes"? They're colorful reminders that we don't have to be perfect in order to persevere.

The Willingness to Risk

Women received back their dead by resurrection. Some were tortured, refusing to accept release, so that they might rise again to a better life. Others suffered mocking and flogging, and even chains and imprisonment. They were stoned, they were sawn in two, they were killed with the sword. They went about in skins of sheep and goats, destitute, afflicted, mistreated—of whom the world was not worthy—wandering about in deserts and mountains, and in dens and caves of the earth.

And all these, though commended through their faith, did not receive what was promised, since God had provided something better for us, that apart from us they should not be made perfect.

Hebrews 11:35-40

Reread Hebrews 11:39-40. In your opinion, what's the difference between heroism and fortitude?

Last summer I was introduced to a very interesting man for a blind date. Mutual friends thought we would make a good pair because we're both outgoing, athletic, and ride Harleys (although I don't like motorcycles enough to have one tattooed on my back like he did). Little did they know he wasn't quite the choirboy he pretended to be!

Anyway, within thirty minutes of my arrival at the mystery man's lake house (which was an hour and a half from Nashville) I started to feel really dizzy. My date seemed genuinely concerned when he asked if I wanted to lie down, but when he started making inappropriate comments, I realized his gratuitousness was nothing more than thinly disguised lust. I don't receive such brazen compliments too often, so I have to admit I was mildly flattered. But I still had enough good sense to hightail it out of there!

> **More Info**
>
> My blind date reminded me of a story I had heard about a single woman contemplating a move to Alaska in the hopes of finding a husband. She asked another woman already living in Fairbanks if the ratio regarding hundreds of available men per every single woman was true. To which the Alaska native replied, "Yeah, the odds are really good . . . but most of the goods are really odd!"

Read Stephen's story in Acts 7. List the tangible ways Stephen stands firm in his faith in the face of certain death. What do you admire the most about his response to this angry, ungodly mob?

Do you think I should get a special chastity award for that? Did my lack of lusty conduct earn me a better husband in the future? No. God isn't a vending machine, granting our wishes when we make good moral choices. Just because I'm attempting to be chaste in my less-than-robust romantic life doesn't mean I'll get a husband with hair and money. In fact, I may never walk down an aisle wearing something borrowed and blue. But while my wedding dreams may never be fulfilled in this lifetime, I must still strive to live in a manner worthy of God. We shouldn't be committed to faithfulness in order to earn good-behavior brownie points. We should be faithful because it brings God divine pleasure.

> *For the grace of God has appeared, bringing salvation for all people, training us to renounce ungodliness and worldly passions, and to live self-controlled, upright, and godly lives in the present age, waiting for our blessed hope, the appearing of the glory of our great God and Savior Jesus Christ, who gave himself for us to redeem us from all lawlessness and to purify for himself a people for his own possession who are zealous for good works.*
>
> Titus 2:11-14

Both Hebrews 11 and Titus 2 have similar themes: We are God's very own people, and our behavior should reflect that beloved status whether or not we receive what was promised.

 **Read Hebrews 11:39 again. Have you ever received a promise from God that has yet to be fulfilled?**

The very Bible we hold in our hands is partly the result of one man's faithfulness, a man who didn't live to see his dream come true. His name was William Tyndale, and he was passionate about translating the Word of God from Greek and Hebrew into English. He wanted common people like us to love and learn from the Holy Scriptures. But Catholic clergy in the early 1500s felt threatened by Tyndale because, as the only "interpreters" of the Scriptures, they were able to manipulate the masses and use God's Word to line their own pockets. They saw Tyndale as a menace who had to be stopped. He fled his home country of England because of threats on his life, but he pressed on to translate two-thirds of the Bible in exile. He was eventually arrested and imprisoned, then ordered to die by strangulation in 1536. In his dying prayer he said, "Lord, open the king of England's eyes."[2] Not long after Tyndale's death, the king did allow the "Great Bible"—largely based on Tyndale's work—to be given to the people. William Tyndale's prayer was answered.

What are you willing to risk in order to be called faithful? What are you willing to give up simply because you're God's very own?

Read Luke 6:22; Matthew 5:10-11; and 1 Peter 4:12-14. Describe the relationship between persecution for Christ's sake and the blessing of God, as well as the relationship between faith and endurance. Share about a time when peace accompanied persecution in your life.

William Tyndale was forty-two years old when he
was martyred. He certainly didn't *receive what was
promised* in his short lifetime. But his death was not
in vain. Neither are the deaths of more than ten
thousand Indonesian Christians who've been
murdered since 1999 by radical Muslims,[3] or the
countless deaths of other believers throughout
history who've paid the ultimate price for their faith
in God—because the Book William Tyndale translated makes it clear that God planned something
better.

**Read 2 Timothy 3:12 and John 15:18-21. What
kind of persecution have you experienced thus
far for your faith in Christ (social/family ridi-
cule, condescension, etc.)? Aside from death,
what kind of *plausible* persecution (something
that's not outside the realm of possibility in our
culture) frightens you the most?**

> *Not one of these people, even though their lives of
> faith were exemplary, got their hands on what was
> promised. God had a better plan for us: that their
> faith and our faith would come together to make
> one completed whole, their lives of faith not
> complete apart from ours.*
>
> Hebrews 11:39-40 (*The Message*)

Regardless of what some preachers promise, all
of our dreams won't necessarily come true in this
life. Just because we send in a check, memorize the
entire New Testament, have perfect church atten-
dance, or fight off the sexual advances of a blind
date, it doesn't mean we'll get fabulous rewards

from heaven here on earth. We probably won't face death by strangulation, but we might die from cancer. We might lose our jobs. We might suffer the disappointment of singleness or divorce or infertility. But just like the Hebrews, we have to learn that this life isn't all there is. This world is not our final resting place.

If you had to give up one of these three things—material comforts or riches, close relationships, or your reputation—for the sake of the gospel, which would be the most difficult for you to lose? Explain.

> We HAVE COME TO THE WRONG STAR. THAT IS WHAT MAKES LIFE AT ONCE SO SPLENDID AND SO STRANGE. THE TRUE HAPPINESS IS THAT WE DON'T FIT. WE COME FROM SOMEWHERE ELSE. WE HAVE LOST OUR WAY.   G. K. CHESTERTON

Read Acts 7:60 and Luke 23:34. Mark Twain wrote, "Forgiveness is the fragrance the flower leaves on the heel that has crushed it." Share an example of when you forgave someone who "crushed" you (and *didn't* say he or she was sorry) for the sake of the gospel.

Running toward
Righteousness

Read Hebrews 12

The 2004 Summer Olympics totally captivated my attention. I love the passion, sportsmanship, and pursuit of excellence the games embody. And that year there were some especially exciting finishes. Paul Hamm—one of the best gymnasts ever to wear red, white, and blue—stumbled in the men's all-around vault competition and almost took out a judge when he careened off the mat. His uncharacteristic mistake appeared to put him totally out of contention for a medal. However, through sheer grit and awe-inspiring athleticism, he clawed his way back to within striking distance by the last rotation. The suspense was palpable when the crowd realized that the fate of this championship would be decided by Paul's final performance.

I was watching the games at home on television—thousands of miles and an ocean away from

Athens, Greece, where they were taking place—and I still had so many butterflies in my stomach that I had to put down my pasta! But Paul Hamm remained totally focused. He calmly walked up to the high bars, executed a near-perfect routine, and stuck his landing. Then when the score was announced and his coach told him he had won the gold medal, his stoicism vanished and he screamed, "No! No!" in ecstatic disbelief. He had just become the first men's all-around Olympic gymnastic champion in American history!

The drama unfolded in similar fashion in the women's all-around gymnastic competition, with U.S. teen sensation Carly Patterson faltering early on, only to charge back later for her own piece of the limelight. And swimmer Michael Phelps had several nail-biting pool duels, as well. Just when it looked like he wouldn't chase down his rivals, he reached for the wall with those impossibly long arms and won yet another of his six gold medals.

But the track and field events are my favorite, probably because I used to run competitively (of course, that term is relative when we're talking about the Olympics). And when twenty-five-year old Fani Halkia, from the host country, Greece, won the 400-meter hurdles and the cheers from her countrymen erupted so loud the stadium seemed to shake, I sobbed as if I knew her personally!

Those epic races were so inspiring that I attempted to recapture a little athletic glory of my own and headed out for a brisk jog in the park. But running with ruptured discs isn't a very good idea, so I ended up wearing a heat pack and gobbling

ibuprofen instead of wearing a wreath and weighing lucrative sponsorship offers.

Read Hebrews 12:1. Who are your personal and public heroes of the faith? How do they cheer you on? If they've passed away, can you picture them cheering you on from glory?

In Hebrews 12:2, when it says, "who for the joy that was set before him endured the cross," the literal Greek translation of the word *for* means "in the place of." In other words, He did it for us! Write a few sentences regarding what it feels like to be referred to as the "joy" Jesus went to the cross for.

The pastor of Hebrews certainly understood the motivational potential of athletic competition. He uses the metaphor of a footrace in chapter 12 in order to encourage his fainthearted team.

> *Therefore, since we are surrounded by so great a cloud of witnesses, let us also lay aside every weight, and sin which clings so closely, and let us run with endurance the race that is set before us, looking to Jesus, the founder and perfecter of our faith, who for the joy that was set before him endured the cross, despising the shame, and is seated at the right hand of the throne of God.* Hebrews 12:1-2

Read Philippians 2:14-16. Who would list *you* as one of the shining stars in their personal cloud of witnesses?

His opening word—"Therefore"—is a significant transitional word reminding the Hebrews that the faithful few they reminisced about in chapter 11 are examples of the blessings that come from living by faith. The pastor dims the lights and puts in the Jacob-to-Jephthah highlight video, telling his discouraged athletes to study the way those who wore their uniforms before them ran. When the tape fades to black, he turns the lights back on and says, "Those guys are cheering for you so loudly in glory, they're shaking the celestial stadium! Now get out there and run the way they did!"

Is there anyone who probably *wouldn't* point to you as an example of someone who loves and trusts God? Why?

Legalism
1. strict adherence, or the principle of strict adherence, to law or prescription, esp. to the letter rather than the spirit.[1]

Then the pastor gives his runners some pointers on improving their racing posture by instructing them to "lay aside every weight, and sin which clings so closely." Bible scholars teach that the word *weight*—which is different from the Greek word used for sin in this verse—refers to the overwhelming burden of the Jewish Levitical system—the burden of the legalistic minutiae they observed in order to "please God."

I enjoyed working as a lifeguard during the summers when I was in high school and college. I liked wearing a bathing suit to work, being paid to get tan, and getting to play the hero to hapless swimmers. Most of the rescues I performed weren't actually for life-threatening situations. Once I had to get a very large, very loud woman unstuck from

her inner tube (Johnson's baby oil was the real hero that afternoon). But every now and then I had to save someone who was in serious trouble. And once I almost went under myself while helping a would-be drowning victim.

I was working at a state park in central Florida called Wekiva Springs, where the water was crystal clear and fifty-eight degrees. We usually had to make several rescues each weekend because, due to the clarity of the spring water, people often didn't realize how deep it was. Or sometimes they just got too cold to swim back to shallow water, which is exactly what happened to a woman one Saturday, right after I had eaten a jumbo chili dog for lunch. The minute I saw her flailing arms and bobbing head, I dove into the water. She was in the deepest part of the natural pool, the area where most of our rescues took place.

When I reached the woman, I put her in a basic lifeguard hold and tried to calm her by assuring her she would be back on dry land in just a few minutes. I had pulled a lot of big swimmers out of this hole before and didn't think a petite dog-paddler would be any problem. But pretty soon I was having a hard time keeping my head above water, too. The woman was so much heavier than I expected. I strained with all my might, chastising myself for eating fair food, and collapsed into a wet heap when we finally made it to shore. That's when the woman's husband—who, unbeknownst to me, had been hanging on to her legs the whole way—sputtered up and began thanking me profusely!

Similarly, the ancient Christians didn't recognize the weight they were still lugging around. Remember, these people came from homes that attempted to cross every *t* and dot every *i* in the law of Moses. They didn't eat cheeseburgers lest they break the "no mixing meat and milk" dietary laws. They didn't mow the yard on the Sabbath, and they sure didn't wear leather Manolos on Yom Kippur.

Much like a sprinter attempting to race in work boots and coveralls, the Hebrews were weighted down by legalism. When they chose to perform rituals instead of pursuing a relationship with Jesus, they suffered spiritual hernias. The load was just too heavy. That's why their pastor tells them to unzip those confining, rigid clothes and run in the freedom Jesus has given them.

What kind of spiritual tracksuit are you wearing?

 Read Philippians 3:7-10 and 1 Corinthians 9:19-23. Has God convicted you of any changes you could make so as to better run the race of faith? (Remember, there's a huge difference between human guilt and the Holy Spirit's conviction!)

The first verse of Hebrews 12 refers to the racecourse itself. We are supposed to "run with endurance the race that is set before us." In other words, we're running on a *fixed course*. I'm sure these ancient believers would have preferred another route—one with less persecution—if they had a

choice in the matter. And most of us are no different. When we get to steep hills or blind curves, we tend to veer off the trail God has marked out for us. But we don't have the option of charting our own course or switching to someone else's because our individual paths are custom-made by our heavenly Father.

Isaiah alludes to this when he teaches about God's graciousness in giving directions:

> *And your ears shall hear a word behind you,*
> *saying, "This is the way, walk in it," when you*
> *turn to the right or when you turn to the left.*
>
> Isaiah 30:21

If we could gallop wherever we wanted, God wouldn't have to tell us which way to turn!

The View from Here

The next part of Hebrews 12 is focused on helping those sluggish athletes finish the race. Their mentor reminds them of Christ's supernatural stamina so they won't throw in the towel:

> *Consider him who endured from sinners such*
> *hostility against himself, so that you may not grow*
> *weary or fainthearted.*   Hebrews 12:3

Read Hebrews 2:10-11 and 12:2-3. What is the pastor teaching his people that's similar about the "founder" of their faith, and what's unique to each passage?

Think about the Son of God, who willingly came to earth, was born in a barn, and lived a perfect life according to the law in order to redeem us from it. Remember what Jesus went through: He was betrayed by His closest friends, convicted in a bogus trial, and nailed to a wooden post to die. Focus on the Founder of your faith: the One who rose again on the third day, ate with His astonished disciples, and then ascended into heaven to sit at the right hand of God and intercede for us. Consider that before whining that you can't run any further.

The most difficult athletic event I've ever competed in involved racing (and I'm using the term loosely here) a bike to the very top of 14,110-foot Pikes Peak in Colorado. The route we climbed is the second highest highway in the world, encompassing 156 turns in twelve miles and ascending more than seven thousand vertical feet. I'll bet the workers who completed that road in 1916 never thought a bunch of masochists on bicycles would attempt to ride it! I trained really hard to prepare for the race, but I was still ready to quit after only a few miles. It was just too long and too hard. My legs felt like cement, and my lungs felt like they were going to burst.

But then I started looking around in an attempt to divert my attention from my aching body. The scenery was spectacular—soaring, snowcapped peaks and high alpine meadows filled with wild-flowers. Pristine lakes were below me, and cute, curious marmots were standing on their hind legs beside the road. Evergreens stood like sentinels, and a surreally blue sky topped off this unbeliev-

able terrarium. I suddenly understood why Kathar-ine Lee Bates was inspired to write "America the Beautiful" after her visit to the summit of Pikes Peak in 1803. The view radically improved my atti-tude and helped me to keep pedaling.

Our view is even more critical when it comes to the spiritual race we're in. If we become preoccu-pied with the difficulties of our current situation or the dreams that have turned to dust or the mean people around us who seem to make out like bandits, we're going to grow weary pretty fast. But if we look toward Jesus, we'll be inspired to keep on keeping on. Our focal point will radically improve our faith.

> Iᴛ's ᴛʜᴇ ʀᴏᴀᴅ sɪɢɴs: "Bᴇᴡᴀʀᴇ ᴏF Lɪᴏɴs."
>
> KIP LAGAT,
> KENYAN DISTANCE COMPETITOR AT THE 2000
> SYDNEY OLYMPICS, EXPLAINING WHY HIS
> COUNTRY PRODUCES SO MANY GREAT RUNNERS

Spaghetti Arms and Jelly Legs

The pastor of Hebrews continues to use the race metaphor, borrowing a page from Isaiah in this next section as he encourages his troops not to let their circumstances get the best of them:

> *Therefore lift your drooping hands and strengthen your weak knees, and make straight paths for your feet, so that what is lame may not be put out of joint but rather be healed.*　　Hebrews 12:12-13

Read Hebrews 12:14-15; Romans 12:14-21; and Ephesians 4:31-32. Which relationships in your

life have been soured by discord or bitterness? Pray for God to reveal any "roots" that need to be pulled from your own heart, then pray for His guidance regarding reconciliation or forgiveness.

> *Strengthen the weak hands, and make firm the feeble knees. Say to those who have an anxious heart, "Be strong; fear not! Behold, your God will come with vengeance, with the recompense of God. He will come and save you."*
>
> Isaiah 35:3-4

The Greek word used for *strengthen* in Hebrews 12 is *anorthoō*, which also means "to restore or rebuild."[2] And I'm so thankful because it denotes God's awareness of our susceptibility to have wimpy arms and jelly legs. He isn't surprised when we whimper and think about quitting. He isn't shocked when we stop running and start walking when we get to a hill in the racecourse. His holy jaw doesn't even drop when we stop walking and plop down on a curb to catch our breath. He simply doesn't give up on us, even when our faithfulness motor needs to be rebuilt!

A COACH CAN BE LIKE AN OASIS IN THE DESERT OF A RUNNER'S LOST ENTHUSIASM.   KEN DOHERTY

You probably remember John the Baptist, Jesus' cousin with a penchant for fur coats and bug casseroles. He was a seriously strong leader who seemed highly unlikely to make mistakes, much less develop spiritual jitters.

John the Baptist was the man chosen by Jehovah to prepare the way for Christ. He was all but above reproach. He took Nazirite vows like Samson (only John kept his!), so he lived a very moral life, basically a monastic existence. Most biblical historians think he spent a lot of time hanging out in Qumran (southeast of Jerusalem) with the Essenes, the guys who wrote the Dead Sea Scrolls. The Essenes were ultraserious about focusing on God, and they didn't have wives or ESPN or anything else to distract them.

As a matter of fact, the Essenes were so reverent about the holiness of God that when they came to the name Jehovah in the Old Testament scrolls they were copying onto parchment and clay tablets, they would literally leave their scroll, take off all their clothes, and rinse themselves in a *mikvah* (a ritual bath) so as to cleanse themselves from impurity. Then they would put on clean clothes and get a new nib for their pen before they sat back down to write God's name.

The Essenes' stoic spirituality gives you just a little insight into the lifestyle of John the Baptist. He was definitely not the type to rededicate his life at youth camp and then go out drinking after a football game. As a matter of fact, John lived such a holy, austere life that many people thought *he* must be the Messiah. If anyone deserved the title of "strong leader" it was John the Baptist. So what happened next probably surprised everyone *except* God:

> *When Jesus had finished instructing his twelve*
> *disciples, he went on from there to teach and preach*

NOTES

in their cities. Now when John heard in prison
about the deeds of the Christ, he sent word by his
disciples and said to him, "Are you the one who is
to come, or shall we look for another?"

Matthew 11:1-3

The gist of John's question was this: "Are you really the Messiah? I mean—good night, Jesus!— I've been out in the desert without a woman, eating locusts and honey, wearing animal skins, and here you are going to parties, hugging lepers, and telling people to love those who persecute them. I thought you were supposed to come spewing fire and all."

And John *had* prophesied that Jesus would come that way before he baptized Him in the Jordan River:

> *I baptize you with water for repentance, but he*
> *who is coming after me is mightier than I, whose*
> *sandals I am not worthy to carry. He will baptize*
> *you with the Holy Spirit and with fire. His*
> *winnowing fork is in his hand, and he will clear*
> *his threshing floor and gather his wheat into the*
> *barn, but the chaff he will burn with unquenchable*
> *fire.*

Matthew 3:11-12

So while I'm obviously taking a little liberty with the Greek, the heart of John the Baptist's query is this: He actually doubts the divinity of Jesus! His race has been long, and he's tired. Plus he's now languishing in a prison cell. His once-sturdy legs have grown weak, and he's about ready to give up.

Jesus could have chastised John. He could have condemned him for his frail faith. Instead, He responds to John's weariness with encouragement:

> *And Jesus answered them, "Go and tell John what you hear and see: the blind receive their sight and the lame walk, lepers are cleansed and the deaf hear, and the dead are raised up, and the poor have good news preached to them. And blessed is the one who is not offended by me."*
>
> Matthew 11:4-6

John was more than familiar with the verses Jesus recited because they were a famous Old Testament prophecy about the coming Messiah. He had probably memorized them when he was a little boy. Elizabeth maybe even cross-stitched them and hung them on his wall, right next to the poster of Moses. Jesus didn't rebuke John for having wimpy arms and jelly legs. As a matter of fact, He even praises John a few verses later, saying that among those born of a woman there was none greater than John the Baptist. Jesus extended mercy in spite of John's jelly legs by graciously reminding him that He was indeed the fulfillment of the prophecies.

Just like John

I once shared this story of John the Baptist at a women's leadership conference. When the conference was over, a woman came up to me in tears. She told me how thankful she was that I had talked about God's great compassion in spite of our weakness rather than the great heights we should aspire to reach. She told me that she would have backed out of the conference if she hadn't already purchased a nonrefundable plane ticket. She said she felt unworthy to be a Christian, much less a Christian *leader*, because her teenage daughter had gotten pregnant and she felt like a bad parent as a result.

She said she had been anxious about the inevitable stares on Sunday morning and the comments behind her back in Bible study. She had been tempted to run and hide rather than "run the race with endurance." And she definitely didn't feel like she deserved to lead others in the race. But through John the Baptist's blunder, God reminded her that He is our constant help in times of trouble. With amazing grace, God led her back out onto the track that day.

Like this woman, like John the Baptist, and like those beleaguered Hebrews, we have to keep putting one foot in front of the other in this race of faithfulness—no matter what happens.

I RAN AND RAN EVERY DAY, AND I ACQUIRED A SENSE OF DETERMINATION, THIS SENSE OF SPIRIT THAT I WOULD NEVER, NEVER, GIVE UP, NO MATTER WHAT ELSE HAPPENED.

WILMA RUDOLPH,
POLIO SURVIVOR AND
TRIPLE GOLD MEDALIST AT THE
1960 OLYMPIC GAMES IN ROME

12

Pardon Me, but Your Faith Is Showing

Read Hebrews 13

As he winds up his encouraging sermon, the pastor of Hebrews slows down to let his flock catch their breath after the inspirational challenge in the previous chapter to keep running. His voice softens, and he smiles warmly at their flushed, attentive faces. Then he gives them a basic outline for what it means to live as a Christian:

Read Hebrews 13:1-3; John 13:34-35; and **3 John 1:5-8. Why do you think a commitment to hospitality was necessary for early Christian efforts and missionaries? Do you think hospitality is as important in modern-day evangelistic efforts? Explain why or why not.**

> *Let brotherly love continue. Do not neglect to show hospitality to strangers, for thereby some have*

entertained angels unawares. Remember those who are in prison, as though in prison with them, and those who are mistreated, since you also are in the body. Let marriage be held in honor among all, and let the marriage bed be undefiled, for God will judge the sexually immoral and adulterous. Keep your life free from love of money, and be content with what you have, for he has said, "I will never leave you nor forsake you."

Hebrews 13:1-5

Read Matthew 25:31-40. Share examples of how you've intentionally extended the type of hospitality reflected in this parable. Has the Holy Spirit impressed upon you to do anything else?

This passage is sort of like a Christianity 101 class syllabus! As believers, we're supposed to:

Love one another well (v. 1)
Extend hospitality (v. 2)
Give grace to persecuted people (v. 3)
Strive for sexual purity (v. 4)
Be content (v. 5)

The simplicity of this salutation reminds me of Elisha's advice to Naaman in 2 Kings:

So Naaman came with his horses and chariots and stood at the door of Elisha's house. And Elisha sent a messenger to him, saying, "Go and wash in the Jordan seven times, and your flesh shall be restored, and you shall be clean." But Naaman was angry and went away, saying, "Behold, I thought

*that he would surely come out to me and stand and
call upon the name of the LORD his God, and wave
his hand over the place and cure the leper. Are not
Abana and Pharpar, the rivers of Damascus, better
than all the waters of Israel? Could I not wash in
them and be clean?" So he turned and went away
in a rage. But his servants came near and said to
him, "My father, it is a great word the prophet has
spoken to you; will you not do it? Has he actually
said to you, 'Wash, and be clean'?" So he went
down and dipped himself seven times in the
Jordan, according to the word of the man of God,
and his flesh was restored like the flesh of a little
child, and he was clean.* 2 Kings 5:9-14

Let's give this story a contemporary spin. Naaman
was a five-star general on a first-name basis with
the king. He was important, privileged, and influ-
ential. But he was also very sick. Although he still
cut a dashing figure in his dress blues, he couldn't
even take off his shirt in front of his wife anymore
because leprosy had caused such horrible disfigure-
ment of his body. When he heard about a man in
Israel who might be able to heal him, Naaman put
on a custom silk suit, waxed his Mercedes, ordered
several soldiers to accompany him, and drove over
en masse to meet Elisha. Children squealed and ran
alongside his entourage; fancy cars and shiny suits
weren't commonplace in that neighborhood. But
Elisha didn't bother to come out of his apartment
to see what all the commotion was about. He just
text-messaged Naaman and told him to perform a
mundane task in a muddy river.

Of course, Naaman was outraged. "How dare this puny Jewish prophet treat me so rudely? He not only snubbed me, he had the audacity to tell me to immerse myself in some nasty ditch! No thank you! I'll just go home and take a bath in my marble tub with surround sound!"

When Naaman pulled up with a posse and a handwritten note from the king (v. 5), he was trying to camouflage his disease with the color of power. He wanted to prove that he was well connected, wielded considerable authority, and could pay handsomely for help. Had Elisha told Naaman to climb a tree next to the Jordan and do a triple-back-layout with two and a half twists into the water, he probably would have agreed without a fight. And he would have saluted those who would have inevitably gathered at the water's edge before he attempted the all-but-impossible dive! But Elisha's prescription wasn't a crowd-pleaser, because Naaman's nerve couldn't heal him. Neither could his connections or cash. Only God could make his skin smooth again.

My guess is that Naaman felt pretty silly when he stood up dripping wet the sixth time. The people onshore were beginning to fold up their chairs and head back home. Watching a man submerge himself over and over again in a dinky creek is boring. No doubt Naaman wished his therapeutic regime was more exciting. Maybe something involving swordplay—he was good at that. But when he came out of the water the seventh time, he didn't question Elisha's simple wisdom anymore!

Living out the fundamentals of our faith won't attract the attention of paparazzi. Television cameras rarely follow believers into prison to record acts of mercy. People don't always acknowledge or applaud when we love them well. And fireworks don't go off when we choose to walk away from a sale instead of buying another silly knickknack for an already crowded shelf. Compassion, grace, and contentment are as difficult to measure as they are for us to put into practice. But we can be sure our heavenly Father notices every inch we move toward being fully satisfied in Him, and He applauds even our tiniest acts of goodness.

> *Whoever gives one of these little ones even a cup of cold water because he is a disciple, truly, I say to you, he will by no means lose his reward.*
>
> Matthew 10:42

Second Semester

After painting a simple but breathtakingly beautiful picture of what Christians should look like, the shepherd of Hebrews adds a few more colors to the canvas:

> *Remember your leaders, those who spoke to you the word of God. Consider the outcome of their way of life, and imitate their faith. Jesus Christ is the same yesterday and today and forever. Do not be led away by diverse and strange teachings, for it is good for the heart to be strengthened by grace, not by foods, which have not benefited those devoted to them. We have an altar from which those who*

serve the tent have no right to eat. For the bodies of those animals whose blood is brought into the holy places by the high priest as a sacrifice for sin are burned outside the camp. So Jesus also suffered outside the gate in order to sanctify the people through his own blood. Therefore let us go to him outside the camp and bear the reproach he endured. For here we have no lasting city, but we seek the city that is to come.

Hebrews 13:7-14

Read Hebrews 13:10-13; Leviticus 4:21 and 16:26-28; and John 19:17-18. Why would the preacher of Hebrews compare the bodies of animals offered on Yom Kippur (the Day of Atonement for practicing Jews) being burned "outside the camp" with Jesus being crucified "outside the gate" of Jerusalem?

As post-postmodern Christians, how can we practically "go outside the camp" of our culture to be with Jesus? How do you wrestle with the concept of not being *of* this world (Romans 12), while living—and loving—*in* this world? Do you think Christians can be "so heavenly minded they're no earthly good"?

Therefore, believers are also supposed to:

Emulate and submit to Christian leadership (v. 7)
Guard good doctrine (vv. 8-9)
Be willing to suffer with Christ (v. 10-13)
Remember that this world isn't our final resting place (v. 14)

Several months ago, I met Debbie Morris. Her name might not ring a bell, but you probably know more about her than you think. A popular movie in the nineties—*Dead Man Walking*, with Sean Penn and Susan Sarandon—was largely based on Debbie's real-life experience. As a teenager, Debbie was innocently enjoying milkshakes with her boyfriend when two convicted felons abducted them at gunpoint. The copy on the cover of her book (*Forgiving the Dead Man Walking*) synopsizes the rest of the story:

> *In the hours that followed, Debbie would experi-*
> *ence atrocities too monstrous to conceive.*
> *Kidnapping, rape, torture, attempted murder . . .*
> *these words cannot convey the horrors that would*
> *continue to poison her life long after her captors*
> *had been brought to justice.*[1]

The woman I met was decades removed from the sixteen-year-old with a sawed-off shotgun pressed against her cheek. She's married to a man named Brad, teaches special education students, and is mommy to two precious children. That terrible night in Louisiana still influences her life, but now the effects are more about hope than horror.

Debbie told me about her personal reaction to the execution of Robert Lee Willie, one of the two perpetrators, in the electric chair. She said she thought she would finally have peace and the whole ordeal would be over once he was put to death. But even after he was gone, she still had a hard time sleeping and some emotional wounds refused to close. It took years for her to understand that justice couldn't give her healing. Then she explained how God had healed her, how He had softened her heart to the point of hoping Robert Lee Willie had repented like the thief on the cross at Golgotha. Her concern for Willie's salvation was amazing. She said that thinking about her own eternity helped her to forgive him for all the suffering he put her through.

Reread Hebrews 13:3 and 10:32-34. Describe another biblical example of how someone who had experienced suffering gave grace to those in the midst of suffering. Has God used past pain in your life to allow you to empathize and extend compassion to others in similar circumstances? If so, explain.

I think that's why the pastor reminds the Hebrews one more time about the way Jesus suffered and encourages them to focus on "the city that is to come." They were living in a world of unspeakable pain and persecution. Suffering had become a way of life, and it was becoming more and more difficult for them to hold on to hope. So he reminds them of home—their real home.

Heaven should be our constant distraction, especially in difficult seasons.

Read Hebrews 13:15. Based on this analogy, our mouths are like *altars* and what comes out of them can be like the *fragrant smoke* from burnt offerings spiraling to God in heaven. Does that

image strike you more as comforting, convicting, or inspiring?

A Blessed Benediction

The pastor's fondness for these Jewish Christians has been evident from the beginning of his sermon, but nowhere is his deep affection for them more apparent than in his parting words:

> *Now may the God of peace who brought again from the dead our Lord Jesus, the great shepherd of the sheep, by the blood of the eternal covenant, equip you with everything good that you may do his will, working in us that which is pleasing in his sight, through Jesus Christ, to whom be glory forever and ever. Amen.* Hebrews 13:20-21

My father attended one of Focus on the Family's Renewing the Heart conferences in Tampa, Florida. It was the first time he had ever heard me speak in public, and it was also the first time he had been in an arena filled with twenty thousand women! He called me afterwards to share what the day meant to him. He told me he had experienced a lot of failure in life—he's been divorced three times and had some difficulties in business—but he said when he watched me talking about Jesus in the middle of that huge auditorium, he knew he must have done something right.

The following are wonderful examples of praise sacrifices in the Psalms: Psalm 4:5; 27:6; 51:15-17; 107:22; and 141:1-2. Which of these

**verses/passages best communicates the fruit of
your lips this past season and why?**

My dad is a kind man, but he's not much of a
talker. So when he told me how proud he was, I
was undone. I still get teary every time I think
about the tender way he affirmed me. That blessed
benediction from him is one of the sweetest gifts
I've ever received.

During this lesson on perseverance, sometimes
the shepherd of Hebrews has had to act like a stern
parent—remember, he even called them hard of
hearing babies and said they needed some big-time
tutoring in order to catch up with God's more
mature kids (Hebrews 5:11-14). But in spite of this
pastor's straightforward admonitions, he always
makes sure his spiritual children don't suffer from
lack of encouragement. His concern for them is
woven throughout his words, and the last thing he
chooses to do is to wrap them in a great big loving
benediction!

**How often do you bless those who consider you
a spiritual parent or mentor?**

**Read Hebrews 13:23. This pastor is obviously
looking forward to being reunited with his
friend and brother in Christ, Timothy. Share
the name of a non-Christian friend or family
member who you would most like to be
reunited with as a believer. Also share specific
prayer needs regarding this person and whether
God could possibly use you to draw that person
to Himself.**

Noisy Pants and Pokey Thumbs

A REAL CHRISTIAN IS AN ODD NUMBER, ANYWAY.
HE FEELS SUPREME LOVE FOR ONE WHOM HE HAS
NEVER SEEN; TALKS FAMILIARLY EVERY DAY TO
SOMEONE HE CANNOT SEE; EXPECTS TO GO TO
HEAVEN ON THE VIRTUE OF ANOTHER; EMPTIES
HIMSELF IN ORDER TO BE FULL; ADMITS HE IS
WRONG SO HE CAN BE DECLARED RIGHT; GOES DOWN
IN ORDER TO GET UP; IS STRONGEST WHEN HE IS
WEAKEST; RICHEST WHEN HE IS POOREST AND
HAPPIEST WHEN HE FEELS THE WORST. HE DIES SO
HE CAN LIVE; FORSAKES IN ORDER TO HAVE; GIVES
AWAY SO HE CAN KEEP; SEES THE INVISIBLE; HEARS
THE INAUDIBLE; AND KNOWS THAT WHICH PASSETH
KNOWLEDGE.   A. W. TOZER

In the introduction of this book, I wrote about a
pastor who asked me to ride his Harley Davidson
down the center aisle of the church in order to stir
up some stiff women in the congregation. I didn't
mention that I wore leather pants during the stunt.
I thought since I was probably going to be black-
balled from retreats everywhere after that wild
ride, I might as well go out with a bang. But the
site of my healthy posterior poured into leather
pants seemed to be even more shocking for some of
those women than the motorcycle!

Plus, those pants caused a disturbance I hadn't
counted on. It's one thing to roar into a sanctuary
on a big bike with fringe streaming from the
handlebars. It's quite another to dismount and
stride toward the podium to the tune of geese being
massacred. I'm sure slender people wearing

animal-skin attire have never had to deal with this particular problem. However, when your dress size is in the double digits, embarrassing noises are just one of the negative consequences of wearing cowhide slacks. Needless to say, it took most people in the audience awhile to take me seriously!

But at the end of the first session, a woman approached me timidly. She smelled like she'd been bathing in cigarettes and had visible tattoos; she certainly didn't fit the stereotype of Christian conference attendee. After we exchanged a few pleasantries, she told me that the only reason she had come to the conference was because a friend from work invited her and wouldn't take no for an answer. She said she hadn't darkened the door of a church for twenty years. She went on to confess some colorful mistakes she had made with men and booze . . . all in a desperate attempt to find a hero. Then she looked down sheepishly, pulled on the hem of her skirt, and said, "I don't know if you can tell, but this is even a borrowed dress. I didn't have anything nice enough to wear to church." I could tell.

She said she almost got up and left before the conference started because she felt so out of place. "But," she said, "then you came in on that Harley and I thought I would stay and see what happened."

We started talking about motorcycles (she and her husband are enthusiasts) and ended up talking about God. She stayed until the very end of the conference, and when I looked over at her during the last song, she was singing with her eyes closed,

her hands raised, and a radiant expression on her face. She looked as if she really believed God loved her, that He was the "hero" she'd been holding out for all these years. There were probably a few women put off by the motorcycle and squeaky pants, but that woman's response was well worth it.

I want to encourage you to run the race God has called us to with authenticity and passion. I'm not advocating that everyone should manifest those qualities by wearing leather pants, but I do think it would behoove some of us to get out of the box we've built to protect our image. This wonderful sermon in Hebrews makes it clear that Christians shouldn't expect to fit in anyway. The Hebrews stuck out like sore thumbs in their world, and we probably should in ours, too!

Scotty Smith, my pastor in Nashville, says, "It's all about *whose* glory and story consumes you." We should be so determined to bring God glory and so devoted to telling His story that our lives stick out awkwardly from the sadness, bitterness, and self-centeredness that define the world in which we live.

We should seek to emulate our heavenly Hero; we should be more loving and more faithful and more gracious and more compassionate and more hopeful than common sense says is possible. We should speak blessings into the lives of our friends, entertain strangers in our homes, be content within our circumstances, have Bible studies in Starbucks, and maybe—just maybe—gladly hop on a motorcycle in order to relate the gospel to one lost sheep!

NOTES

What was your favorite chapter—or passage—of Hebrews during this study and why? If you could ask the preacher of Hebrews just one question, what would it be?

Introduction

[1]"Holding Out for a Hero" from the Paramount Motion Picture *Footloose*. Words by Dean Pitchford. Music by Jim Steinman. Copyright © 1984 by Ensign Music Corporation. International copyright secured. All rights reserved.

Chapter 1: Danger Ahead

[1] *Dictionary of New Testament Backgrounds*, eds. Craig A. Evans and Stanley E. Porter (Downers Grove, Ill.: InterVarsity Press, 2000), 969.

[2] Edward Gibbon, *The History of the Decline and Fall of the Roman Empire*, abridged ed. (London: Penguin Books, Ltd., 2000), 135.

[3] Ibid., 169. Also from class lecture and syllabus notes from "Hebrews to Revelation," taught by Daniel Doriani, Ph.D., Covenant Seminary, St. Louis, Missouri.

[4] Justo L. Gonzalez, *The Story of Christianity*, Vol. 1, *The Early Church to the Dawn of the Reformation* (New York: HarperCollins, 1984), 33–36.

Chapter 2: The Beginning of the "Better Than's"

[1]William L. Lane, *Hebrews: A Call to Commitment* (Eugene, Ore.: Wipf and Stock, 1985), 15–26.

[2]Warren W. Wiersbe, *Be Confident: Live by Faith, Not by Sight* (Colorado Springs: Victor Publishing, 2003), 21–32.

[3]J. Julius Scott, *Jewish Backgrounds of the New Testament* (Grand Rapids, Mich.: Baker Books, 1995), 32-33, 39.

[4]Scott, *Jewish Backgrounds*, 252–254.

Chapter 3: Drifting Away Again

[1] John MacArthur, *The MacArthur Study Bible* (Nashville: Word, 1997), 1898.

[2] *Hebrew-Greek Key Word Study Bible* (Chattanooga, Tenn.: AMG, 1996), 1408, 2118.

Chapter 4: People Don't Deserve Pedestals

[1] Justo L. Gonzalez, *The Story of Christianity*, Vol. 2, *The Reformation to the Present Day* (New York: HarperCollins, 1985), 51–53.

[2] www.annabelle.net/topics/fame.php

[3] Jennifer Wulff, et al., "Pressure to Be Perfect: The Heat Is on Young Celebs to Look Thinner and Sexier than Ever—and Their Fans Will Do Almost Anything to Be Just Like Them," *People*, 26 July 2004, 72–78.

Chapter 5: Busyness Isn't a Spiritual Gift

[1] *Webster's Encyclopedic Unabridged Dictionary* (New York: Random House, 1996), 1885.

[2] Ibid., 1641.

[3] John MacArthur, *The MacArthur Study Bible* (Nashville: Word, 1997), 1902.

Chapter 6: The Certainty of God's Calling

[1] *Hebrew-Greek Key Word Study Bible* (Chattanooga, Tenn.: AMG, 1996), 1411, 1683.

[2] Wayne Grudem, *Systematic Theology* (Grand Rapids, Mich.: Zondervan, 1994), 789.

[3] Ibid., 791.

Chapter 7: A Man Named Mel

[1] John MacArthur, *The MacArthur Study Bible* (Nashville: Word, 1997), 1625.

Chapter 8: Red Is the Color of Redemption

[1] Bill Arnold and Bryan Beyer, *Encountering the Old Testament* (Grand Rapids, Mich.: Baker, 1999), 94.

[2] Words and music by Lewis E. Jones, public domain.

Chapter 9: Torn Curtains and True Friends

[1] John MacArthur, *The MacArthur Study Bible* (Nashville: Word, 1997), 1903.

[2] *I Thought My Father Was God: And Other True Stories from NPR's National Story Project*, ed. Paul Auster (New York: Henry Holt, 2001), 226.

[3] John Eldredge, *Waking the Dead* (Nashville: Nelson, 2003), 191.

[4] Ibid., 198.

Chapter 10: Misfits, Martyrs, and Miracles

[1] *International Standard Bible Encyclopedia*, James Orr, general ed., "Sorek, Valley of" www.studylight.org

[2] William Tyndale, *A Letter from Prison*, from Archives du Rotaume Belgique.

[3] *The Voice of the Martyrs' Newsletter*, September 2003.

Chapter 11: Running toward Righteousness

[1] *Webster's Encyclopedic Unabridged Dictionary* (New York: Random House, 1996), 1098.

[2] *Hebrew-Greek Key Word Study Bible* (Chattanooga, Tenn.: AMG, 1996), 2055.

Chapter 12: Pardon Me, but Your Faith Is Showing

[1] Debbie Morris with Gregg Lewis, *Forgiving the Dead Man Walking* (Grand Rapids, Mich.: Zondervan, 1998), book jacket.